Finding Legal Information

A guide to print and electronic sources

DAVID PESTER

Chandos Publishing

Oxford · England · New Hampshire · USA

Contents

Indexes

Introduction

Law students and lawyers used to be dependent on the library to use the law reports and statutes (and photocopiers) in it. The law has always changed daily and students have always struggled to buy many textbooks. But now they have a wealth of other sources, including databases and the Internet, they can use, so they are not tied to the library in the same way. These resources can often be accessed from home and can save considerable time and money. However, that wealth can be confusing – what is the best and most authoritative source is not always clear and access to technology and costly databases is still variable.

This book is intended as a practical and straightforward guide to legal information sources, covering those that are the most up-to-date, both printed and electronic. It is meant to be an accessible and easy-to-use directory of legal information sources for librarians, lawyers, students and anyone needing legal information.

The emphasis is on British and European law, starting with general material, including case law and statutes, journals and reference material such as dictionaries, directories and research guides. The focus then moves to the main legal topics, followed by an appendix listing the legal publishers mentioned in the text and Internet bookshops. Lastly there are indexes of online services and websites and title and author indexes, while a list of the abbreviations used throughout is provided at the front of the book.

The aim is to be as comprehensive and up-to-date as possible, taking in important legal developments such as civil procedure reform, devolution and human rights law and encompassing the explosion of information on the web and the availability of online services.

Textbooks are mentioned which are well established and current. Sufficient details to identify them are included and an ISBN is provided (preference being given to that for the paperback).

Material specially written for Legal Practice students has not been included. There are a number of widely available series for these, issued annually, such as the Legal Practice course guides from Oxford University Press (previously issued by Blackstone Press) and the LPC series published by Jordans with the College of Law.

Relevant electronic sources are included, with details of scope and any limitations of coverage. If an Internet link listed in the book has changed, try the home page if appropriate or use the site's search engine, if it has one, to track the page down.

List of abbreviations

AC	Appeal Cases (law reports) or Appeal Court
ACAS	Arbitration, Conciliation and Advisory Service
ACD	Administrative Court Digest
Admin LR	Administrative Law Reports
AJIL	American Journal of International Law
All ER	The All England Law Reports
All ER Rep	The All England Law Reports Reprint
All ER Rev	The All England Law Reports Annual Review
ALT	Association of Law Teachers
APIL	Association of Personal Injury Lawyers
AUSTLII	Australian Legal Information Institute
BAILII	British and Irish Legal Information Institute
BCC	British Company Cases
BCLC	Butterworths Company Law Cases
BIALL	British and Irish Association of Law Librarians
BIPR Online	Bankruptcy and Personal Insolvency Reports Online
BOPCAS	British Official Publications Current Awareness Service
BSD	Busy Solicitors' Digest
BTC	British Tax Cases
BTR	British Tax Review
BYBIL	British Yearbook of International Law
CA	Court of Appeal

CALIM	Current Awareness for Legal Information Managers
Can YBIL	Canadian Yearbook of International Law
CCA	Court of Criminal Appeal
Ch	Chancery Division (law reports)
CLI	Current Legal Information
CLJ	Cambridge Law Journal
CLP	Current Legal Problems
CLRT	Current Legal Research Topic
CLS	Current Law Statutes
CLYB	Current Law Year Book
Cm	Command papers since 1986
CMLR	Common Market Law Reports
Comp Law	The Company Lawyer
Conv	The Conveyancer and Property Lawyer
Court Forms	Atkin's Encyclopaedia of Court Forms in Civil Proceedings (2nd edn)
Cox CC	Cox's Criminal Law Cases
Cr App R	Criminal Appeal Reports
Crim LR	Criminal Law Review
CPR	Civil Procedure Rules
CPS	Crown Prosecution Service
D	The Digest
DPP	Director of Public Prosecutions
EC	European Community
ECHR	European Court of Human Rights
ECJ	European Court of Justice
EcomHR	European Commission of Human Rights
ECR	European Court Reports
EG	Estates Gazette

EGLR	Estates Gazette Law Reports
EHRLR	European Human Rights Law Review
EHRR	European Human Rights Reports
EIN	Electronic Immigration Network
EIPR	European Intellectual Property Review
EJIL	European Journal of International Law
ELR	European Law Review
ELR Online	Education Law Reports Online
ELSA	European Law Students Association
EMLR	Entertainment and Media Law Reports
Env LR	Environmental Law Reports
ER	English Reports
EU	European Union
F	Family Division (law reports)
Fam Law	Family Law (journal)
FCSC	Financial Services Compensation Scheme
FLR	Family Law Reports
FLR Online	Family Law Reports Online
Forms & Precedents	Encyclopaedia of Forms and Precedents (5th edn)
FSA	Financial Services Authority
FSR	Fleet Street Reports
HC	High Court
HL	House of Lords
HLR	Harvard Law Review
HRA	Human Rights Act
IALS	Institute of Advanced Legal Studies
ICJ	International Court of Justice
ICLQ	International and Comparative Law Quarterly

ICLR	Incorporated Council of Law Reporting for England and Wales
ICR	Industrial Cases Reports
IIC	International Review of Industrial Property and Copyright Law
IJLT	International Journal of Law and Information Technology
IJRL	International Journal of Refugee Law
ILEX	Institute of Legal Executives
ILM	International Legal Materials
ILR	International Law Reports
Imm AR	Immigration Appeals
Ind LJ	Industrial Law Journal
Info TLR	Information Technology Law Reports
INLR Online	Immigration and Nationality Law Reports Online
IPPC	Integrated Pollution Prevention and Control
IRLR	Industrial Relations Law Reports
JBL	Journal of Business Law
JCL	Journal of Criminal Law
JCLLE	Journal of Commonwealth Law and Legal Education
JIBL	Journal of International Banking Law
JICJ	Journal of International Criminal Justice
JILT	Journal of Information Law and Technology
JLH	Journal of Legal History
JR	The Juridical Review
L&TR	Landlord and Tenant Reports
Law Com	Law Commission Reports
LJR	The Law Journal Reports
Lloyd's Rep	Lloyd's Law Reports

LLP	limited liability partnership
LLR Online	Licensing Law Reports Online
LQR	Law Quarterly Review
LR	Law Reports
LS	Legal Studies: The Journal of the Society of Legal Studies; the Law Society
LT	Law Times Reports
MLR	Modern Law Review
NLJ	New Law Journal
Nott LJ	Nottingham Law Journal
Oftel	Office of Telecommunications
OISC	Office of the Immigration Services Commissioner
OJ Eur Comm	Official Journal of the European Communities
OJLS	Oxford Journal of Legal Studies
P&CR	Property, Planning and Compensation Reports
PGO	Public Guardianship Office
PL	Public Law (journal)
PNLR	Professional Negligence and Liability Reports
QB	Queen's Bench Division (law reports)
RPC	Reports of Patent, Design and Trade Mark Cases
RTR	Road Traffic Reports
SC	Supreme Court
SEPA	Scottish Environment Protection Agency
SI	Statutory Instrument
SJ	Solicitors Journal
SLS	The Society of Legal Studies
SLR	Statute Law Review
SLT	Scots Law Times
SOSIG	Social Science Information Gateway

SR & O	Statutory Rules and Orders
STC	Simon's Tax Cases
TLR	Times Law Reports
TSO	The Stationery Office
UK	United Kingdom
UKHRR	UK Human Rights Reports
UKHRR Online	UK Human Rights Reports Online
UN	United Nations
WLR	The Weekly Law Reports
YBEL	Yearbook of European Law
YLJ	Yale Law Journal

About the author

David Pester has worked for some seventeen years in libraries, mainly academic. He studied law at the University of Kent at Canterbury and worked at the Institute of Advanced Legal Studies and House of Lords Library before taking his current job at City Campus, London Metropolitan University (previously London Guildhall University prior to the merger with the University of North London).

As well as working in cataloguing, David enjoys helping law students find the material they want, understand the sources and use the electronic resources. He has chaired courses on legal materials for new law librarians.

David brings to this book knowledge of the law and legal materials, academic libraries and enquiry work, together with a cataloguer's insistence on the need for accurate references.

The author may be contacted via the publisher.

Part 1

General and Primary Material

Primary and secondary material explained

Fundamental to United Kingdom legal literature is the split between primary sources, the law itself, and secondary sources, being commentary on the law.

Primary sources are the original and authoritative statements of the law, consisting of legislation made by Parliament and case law, the judgments and decisions made by the courts.

Legislation further splits into primary and secondary or delegated legislation. Essentially, primary legislation is made up of Acts of Parliament. These statutes are legal rules on a particular subject, which have usually been passed by the two Houses of Parliament and received royal assent to become law. Public General Acts apply to the whole jurisdiction and can be contrasted with Local Acts which apply to certain areas only and Personal Acts which are for certain people and their estates only.

It is often worth also studying Bills, although they are only draft versions of proposed Acts and are superseded by the Acts themselves once given royal assent. Current Bills reveal what is being proposed but it can also be illuminating to look at the various, sometimes substantial, changes made to a Bill as it goes through Parliament.

Secondary or delegated legislation consists of statutory instruments, statutory rules and orders, orders in council, codes of practice, by-laws and measures of the Synod of the Church of England. Statutes lay out Parliament's general intention in a particular field and the secondary legislation is made under powers conferred by Acts to fill in the detail, setting out exactly how they will work.

To study legislation well, it is necessary to know how to find Bills, look for a particular statute, and check if a statute is in force, has been amended or repealed. You will also want to be able to do a subject search to find out what legislation affects a particular area of the law. You will also want to find relevant statutory instruments.

The other primary source is case law, the decisions of judges built up over centuries. It is necessary to know about the main law report series, understand how citations work, how to find a report where you only have part of the reference and how to find cases on a particular subject. You will also need to check whether a case has been judicially considered, that is applied or overruled by a subsequent case. For both legislation and case law, you have to decide when it is best or easiest to use the print sources or to make use of one of the online sources.

Secondary sources are also important, but they have a supporting role in relation to primary sources, providing commentary on and explanation of the actual law. They are made up of textbooks, a range of established academic works, casebooks and statute books, encyclopaedic and practitioner works, legal journals and reference materials, including directories, citators and dictionaries. These sources are backed up by relevant websites and the online current awareness services.

Fundamental to successful legal research, whether by practitioners or students, is the need for authoritative and completely up-to-date sources of law. With the wealth of choice available today and many online services being updated daily, there is no excuse for not knowing the latest position, but the sheer amount of sources can still make it a daunting task.

Primary material

Law reports

The reports

The All England Law Reports. London: Butterworths (All ER).

Covers cases in the House of Lords, Privy Council, Court of Appeal and all divisions of the High Court since 1936. Has a weekly issue, a current table and index issued four times a year, a cumulative index at the end of the year and consolidated tables and index every three years. The cumulative and consolidated indexes include cases reported and considered, statutes considered and subject indexes. There is also a noter-up service, which provides labels indicating if a case is still current law. There are cross-references in the reports to other works published by Butterworths, including *Halsbury's Laws*, *Halsbury's Statutes*, *Halsbury's Statutory Instruments* and *The Digest*.

Also available as a CD-Rom and as an online subscription.

The All England Law Reports Reprint. London: Butterworths (All ER Rep).
ISBN: 0406996280 (set).

Like the *English Reports*, this covers early authorised reports, cases spanning 1558–1935. It has an index.

English Reports. Edinburgh: Green; London: Stevens, 1925 (ER).

Before the *Law Reports* began in 1865, most law reports were compiled by individuals and were known by the name of the compiler. These are known as nominate reports and most of them are reprinted in the *English Reports*. This is an excellent way to find old cases. The whole series and indexes are available on CD-Rom (Cape Town: Jutaset, 1998).

If you know the name of the case you want, use the two index volumes. These include the original citation and the reference to the volume number and page number for the *English Reports*. To find the case, it is easier to use the pagination on the outside margin of the reports rather than the original pagination for the nominate report. For example, the citation *Orr v. Churchill* 1 H BL 226 126 131 means that this case was originally in volume 1 of *Blackstone's Common Pleas Reports* and is reprinted in volume 126 of the *English Reports* at page 131 (the number on the outside margin).

If you only have a citation to the original series and not the case name, then it is a bit harder. You will have to find the full name of the report by looking in Raistrick, Donald, *Index to Legal Citations and Abbreviations* (2nd edn) (see p. 42) and then look up the name in the Index chart for the *English Reports*, which will tell you which volume of the *English Reports* the case is in. The chart lists the original series, the volume in the *English Reports*, the abbreviation of the original series and the approximate period covered. Then go through the volume to find the report, checking the original pagination for the nominate report, which is found on the inside margin.

For example, if all you have is 5 Moo 82, then you will have to find out that this abbreviation is for *E.F. Moore's Privy Council Reports*. Look this series up in the chart for the *English Reports* and you will see that volumes 3–7 of *Moore's Privy Council Reports* are in volume 13 of the *English Reports*. Look through this volume to locate page 82 of volume 5 of Moore's, checking the inside margin and you will find that this case starts on page 421 (outside margin) of the *English Reports*.

The Law Journal Reports. London: Ince (LJR).

Continued *Law Journals: New Series*, spanning 1832–1947 and was then absorbed itself by *The All England Reports*.

Law Reports. Incorporated Council of Law Reporting for England and Wales (LR).

These are still the reports preferred by the courts ahead of the other reports and are written by barristers for the Incorporated Council of Law Reporting for England and Wales. The Council's writers also contribute cases to the companion series, *The Weekly Law Reports* and to *The Times, Solicitors Journal* and Law Society's *Gazette.*

The reports started in 1865 and since 1895 the volumes have been divided into the following courts:

- Appeal Cases (AC)
- Chancery Division (Ch)
- Probate (now Family) Division (F)
- Queen's (or King's) Bench Division (QB).

The *Law Reports* cumulative and consolidated indexes (*The Pink Index* and *The Red Index* respectively) are explained on pp. 9–10. The reports are also supported by a free Internet service *The Daily Law Notes* (*http://www .law reports.co.uk*) (see p. 15).

The *Law Reports* are also available as a CD-Rom, on *The Justis Databases* (p. 14) and on other online services such as *Westlaw UK* (p. 35).

The Law Times Reports: Containing All the Cases Argued and Determined in the House of Lords ... London: H. Cox (LT).

Lloyd's Law Reports. London: Informa Professional. 0024-5488 (Lloyd's Rep).

Covers maritime and commercial law. Has accompanying citator. Continues *Lloyd's List Law Reports*. Available on *Westlaw.*

Scots Law Times. Edinburgh: W. Green (SLT).

Issued every Friday during court times, with 40 issues a year. Has case reports from all Scottish courts, case commentaries, articles and book reviews, new court rules and practice directions.

It is also available as a monthly CD-Rom and on *Westlaw.* Selected items from the news section are on the publisher's site (*http://www.wgreen.co.uk*).

The Times Law Reports. London: Times Publishing (TLR).

Until 1950, the reports from the newspaper written by reporters from the Incorporated Council of Law Reporting were published in this series.

The Times Law Reports. Edinburgh: T. & T. Clark. ISSN: 0958-0441.

Monthly and annual volumes from 1990 onwards. Very recent reports from *The Times* and other newspapers can be found on *LexisNexis Executive* (see p. 35) or on the websites *Times Online* and *The Times Legal Archive* (see p. 16). There is also *The Justis Databases* online service, *Times Law Reports* (see p. 14).

The Weekly Law Reports. London: Incorporated Council of Law Reporting for England and Wales. ISSN: 0019-3518 (WLR).

Started in 1953, *The Weekly Law Reports*, the companion series to the *Law Reports*, are published 45 times a year, covering developments in superior and appellate courts.

Each year is divided into three volumes: volume 1 has cases which do not warrant inclusion in the *Law Reports*, while volumes 2 (January–June) and 3 (July–December) have cases which will be later published in the *Law Reports* with a note of counsel's argument. Cases in the Law Society's *Gazette* marked WLR will be published in *The Weekly Law Reports*.

The *Law Reports* pink and red indexes (see Finding tools below) cover *The Weekly Law Reports* and the reports are supported by a free Internet service *The Daily Law Notes* (see p. 15).

The Weekly Law Reports are available on *The Justis Databases* (see p. 14).

Finding tools particularly applicable to cases

The All England Law Reports Annual Review. London: Butterworths (All ER Rev).

Issued with *The All England Law Reports*, this is a collection of articles evaluating significant cases (with citations) in human rights, statute law, European Union law and particular subject areas.

All England Legal Opinion. London: Butterworths

Ten issues a year with *The All England Law Reports* focus on case comment and case abstracts.

Current Law Case Citator. London: Sweet & Maxwell

Excellent way of finding a case if you have the name but not the full reference. The volumes cover cases from 1947 and are split by date.

It also has a list of legal abbreviations.

Available as online service *Current Legal Information* (see p. 32).

The Digest: Annotated British, Commonwealth and European Cases. London: Butterworths. ISBN: 0406025002 (for set) (D).

Originally published as *English and Empire Digest* in 49 volumes between 1919 and 1932, *The Digest* has abstracts of cases. It consists of replacement volumes, subject indexes, consolidated tables of cases and annual supplements. The quarterly survey has cases subsequent to the annual supplement, arranged by title, with a list of new cases and cases judicially considered.

The Digest is a very useful source, but it is very cumbersome to use and it is worth looking at the user's guide for help. To find a case, you look in the consolidated tables of cases and then are referred onto the appropriate volume number. You have to search the table of cases for that volume, which gives you the page or case number at which the report appears.

The *Law Reports* indexes

The Law Reports Cumulative Index. London: Incorporated Council of Law Reporting for England and Wales.

Known as *The Pink Index*, this covers cases reported in *Industrial Cases Reports*, *The All England Law Reports*, *The All England Commercial Cases*, *The All England European Cases*, *Criminal Appeal Reports*, *Lloyd's Law Reports*, *Local Government Reports*, *Road Traffic Reports* and *Simon's Tax Cases* as well as *The Weekly Law Reports* and the *Law Reports* themselves. It is possible to search by case name to find a citation and to search by subject.

The Pink Index also has lists of cases judicially considered (this is not limited to cases in the headnotes of the reports) and statutes, statutory instruments, European Community enactments, overseas enactments and international conventions judicially considered. To be sure of being completely up to date, it is necessary to check in subsequent issues of *The Weekly Law Reports*.

The Law Reports Digest. London: Incorporated Council of Law Reporting for England and Wales.

There are short abstracts of cases from 1865 to 1950, arranged by general subject headings.

Law Reports Index. London: Incorporated Council of Law Reporting for England and Wales.

Known as *The Red Book* or *The Red Indexes*, this consolidates *The Pink Index* and covers the same law reports. It has all cases since 1951. Cases are arranged by title and subject and the headings can be checked here to see which is best to search in *The Pink Index*.

Finding cases in the print sources

Understanding citations

If you know the full citation of the case you want and what it stands for, then you can go straight to the law report. However, it is worth understanding the elements that make up the citation.

The citation has four elements: abbreviation of the title of the report, date, volume number and the page number of the beginning of the case report. The date is normally in square brackets and is the year in which the case was reported. For example, *Cadogan v. Dimovic* [1984] 2 All ER 168 means that the case is to be found on page 168 of the second volume for 1984 of *The All England Law Reports*. However, if the reports have running volume numbers regardless of year, then the date is in round brackets and is the year judgment was given. An example of this is *Wills v. Bowley* (1982) 75 Cr App R 164, which is in the 75th volume of the *Criminal Appeal Reports* at page 164. In this instance, the date is not essential to finding the right report.

The form of citation for the *Law Reports* has changed over the years, illustrating this point about the date:

- *1865–1875*, e.g. *Cooper v. Phibbs* (1867) LR 3 HL 149 – this is from volume 3 of the English and Irish Appeals (House of Lords).
- *1876–1890*, e.g. *Thomas v. Quartermaine* (1887) 18 QB 685 – this is in volume 18 of the Queen's Bench Division.
- *1891* onwards, e.g. *Jacques v. Owners of Steam Tug Alexandra* [1921] 2 AC 339 – this is in volume 2 of the Appeal Cases for 1921 at page 339.

If the author of a textbook or article wants to highlight a particular page of a report for study, then they will give the citation with the first page of the case and then add 'at xxx' (the page they want to mention), e.g. *Pelling v. Pelling* [1998] 1 FSR 636 at 652.

If you do not know what the citation means, e.g. what LJR is, then check one of these lists of abbreviations:

- Raistrick, Donald. *Index to Legal Citations and Abbreviations* (2nd edn). Published in 1993, this is still the best to try first.
- *Halsbury's Laws of England*. List of references and abbreviations in Vol. 1(1).
- *Current Law Case Citator*. List at the beginning.
- *Current Law Year Book* also has a short list of common abbreviations.
- *The Digest*. The preliminary pages of the cumulative supplement have abbreviations.

If you know the name of the case you want but not the whole citation, then look it up in the following indexes. Start with *Current Law Case Citator* for cases since 1947. Try each volume in turn (they are split by date). If the case is earlier than 1865, then look up the case in the index to the *English Reports*, which is likely to have the case. Many law reports have their own index, including *The All England Law Reports* and the *Law Reports*, which has an index covering *The Weekly Law Reports* and other reports too. *Halsbury's Laws of England* has a case index. *The Digest* has comprehensive case indexes, but is difficult to use and it is easier to try the other sources first. For very recent cases, it is best to check the latest *Current Law Monthly Digest* (see p. 43), the most recent cumulative index to *The All England Law Reports* or *Law Reports* and the table of cases in the most up-to-date *The Weekly Law Reports*.

Searching by subject

If you do not have a particular case to look up but want to find cases on a particular topic, then you need to check under the subject headings in the following reference works or look in their subject index:

- *Halsbury's Laws of England*. The volumes are arranged by subject and there is a good subject index.
- *The Digest*. Subject searches are easy in this too by going directly to the volume for the subject required or using the index where you can pinpoint the exact aspect of the topic you want.
- *Current Law Year Book* includes abstracts of cases and a search in this should be combined with one in *Current Law Monthly Digest* for the latest cases.

Digests and indexes to individual law reports include subject indexes as well as those arranged by case name.

Recent textbooks, casebooks and updated loose-leaf works on a particular subject are another source of references.

Up-to-date information

When you do a search, it is essential that you check for the very latest information to make sure the law has not recently changed and you are not missing an important case. To check if a case has been considered, distinguished or followed, then look in the *Current Law Case Citator* and *Monthly Digest* or in the index to the *Law Reports* or *The Digest*.

The online services most relevant to case law are considered next and obviously are very much alternatives to the print sources we have been discussing, or can also be used in combination with them. In particular, the online current awareness services, such as *Lawtel* and *New Law Online*, are good ways of preventing research being out of date.

Online services

These are the services most recommended for case law. There is a further list of general online services on p. 31 and law reports on a particular subject are in Part 2. You can generally search by keyword or free text to find cases on a particular subject and limit your search by date. Once you have found a relevant case, you can see what subject terms have been used and look for further relevant cases by using these. Where you are looking for a particular case, you can search using all or part of the party names. Moreover, it is possible to look for all cases involving a particular judge or counsel.

All England Direct

Part of *Butterworths LexisNexis Direct Services* (see p. 31), this has all of the *All England Law Reports*, with cross-references to other major legal works published by Butterworths, including *Halsbury's Laws*, *Halsbury's Statutes and Statutory Instruments* and *The Digest*. Includes decisions of the European Courts.

For more information, see *http://www.lexisnexis.co.uk/All_England-Direct.asp.*

CaseSearch

Also part of *Butterworths LexisNexis Direct Services*, this has details of English, Irish, Scottish and Commonwealth cases, not full text, with alternative citations and procedural history. It is regularly updated.

The Law Reports and *Weekly Law Reports* (*The Justis Databases* (see p. 33)).

Complete sets of both reports are on the one database, replacing *Electronic Law Reports*. The original page numbers from the reports are included.

Law Reports Online

From Jordans and Family Law by subscription, an online library of their specialist law reports. Includes:

- *Bankruptcy and Personal Insolvency Reports Online (BIPR Online)*
- *Education Law Reports Online (ELR Online)*
- *Family Law Reports Online (FLR Online)*
- *Immigration and Nationality Law Reports Online (INLR Online)*
- *Licensing Law Reports Online (LLR Online)*
- *United Kingdom Human Rights Reports Online (UKHRR Online)*.

Law Reports Online also offers an e-mail case alert service.
For more information, see *http://www.lawreportsonline.co.uk*.

Lawtel (see p. 34)

Excellent current awareness service, with the full text of cases since 1980.

LexisNexis Professional (see p. 34)

Has a very wide-range of law reports.

New Law Online (see p. 35)

Has the full judgment of cases within 48 hours.

Times Law Reports (*The Justis Databases*)

Has full text of the reports from 1990 and since September 2001 the reports have been enhanced by case summaries prepared by barrister John Cooper.

Westlaw UK (see p. 35)

Huge number of law reports, including many of Sweet & Maxwell's specialist series.

Websites

These are Internet sources most relevant to case law (see p. 36 for general websites).

The Daily Law Notes (*http://www.lawreports.co.uk*)

Useful free service, complementing the *Law Reports* and *The Weekly Law Reports*, which has precise summaries of key cases within 24 hours of judgment. These will later appear in *The Weekly Law Reports*.

House of Lords Judicial Work and Judgments (*http://www.parliament .the-stationery-office.co.uk/pa/ld/ldjudinf.htm*)

Includes House of Lords judgments since November 1996 and has details of their judicial work, a list of Law Lords and civil practice and criminal practice directions.

Smith Bernal (*http://www.smithbernal.com*)

This is the site of the official transcribers Smith Bernal and is a very useful source of reported cases. The casebase is a free transcript archive, with over 20,000 cases from the Court of Appeal and Administrative Court (previously the Crown Office). It is possible to search by case, date, case number and Division.

Swarb.co.uk (*http://www.swarb.co.uk* (see also p. 41))

This is an excellent site, with *Cases Lawindex*, an index for references to all cases in *The Times*, and the legal update section of the Law Society's *Gazette* from January 1992. The *Gazette* entries cover *The Weekly Law Reports* and the *Estates Gazette*. The index also covers reports in *The Independent* from

1993 to 1996. As reporters from *The All England Law Reports* prepared these reports, this is the equivalent of a search in those reports for that period. From March 2001, links from the index to the full text of the case are being added. The aim is to be up to date within two weeks.

Times Law Reports on **Times Online** (*http://www.timesonline.co.uk*)

The Times Law Reports are on *The Times* website for free for seven days after publication. They are then on *The Times Legal Archive*.

The Times Legal Archive (*http://www.lawreports.newsint-archive.co.uk*)

This web-based subscription service has *The Times Law Reports* back to 1985 and law articles from May 1989.

Neutral citations for electronic and printed reports

Courts are becoming aware of the electronic sources of law reports. A practice direction by Lord Woolf in 2001 said that it was permissible to cite a judgment in court that was reported in a series of reports by using a copy of the judgment in electronic form that has been authorised by the publisher of the original series. The *Law Reports* are still preferred over other series, whether in their electronic or print version.

That practice direction, Lord Woolf, *Judgments: Form and Neutral Citation* CA, 11 January 2001, introduced a new neutral form of citation, so cases will have a reference number and paragraph numbers which are the same in electronic or printed reports. For example, the neutral citation for the case *Holland* v. *Burnett* is *Holland* v. *Burnett* [2001] EWCA Civ 10. These official vendor and media neutral citations are designed to aid publication of judgments on the Internet and to help people using online services. A further practice direction, The Lord Chief Justice of England and Wales, *Neutral Citations*, 14 January 2002, extended the use of neutral citations, so most United Kingdom courts are now assigning them. The various indexes that have been discussed are listing the neutral citation as well as the citation from the printed series.

Statutes, Bills, statutory instruments

Statutes

Current Law Statutes. London: Sweet & Maxwell (CLS).

Annotated versions of the statutes, with annual bound volumes arranged by date and supported by service volumes. The annotations and notes are very useful, explaining the meaning of words and phrases in a statute, summarising the provisions and explaining the relationship of the Act to earlier statutes and cases. The service volumes include current statutes, but they may only appear in this publication some time after the Stationery Office has published them individually.

Halsbury's Statutes of England and Wales (4th edn). London: Butterworths. ISBN: 0406949638 (for set).

Supported by cumulative supplements, a current service, a noter-up service, tables of statutes and a consolidated index. The volumes are arranged by subject in a similar way to *Halsbury's Laws* and the statutes are annotated. Use the detailed subject index to find the Act you want. *Halsbury's Statutes* is a source for pre-1900 statutes which are still in force. The current statutes service binder has annotated versions of statutes published in this year, but as with *Current Law Statutes*, there is a delay in publication.

The Public General Acts and Measures. London: Stationery Office.

Publishing statutes from 1871, the official series has the Acts without annotations or any amendments. There are normally two annual volumes and the statutes are in chapter number order. The General Synod Measures of the Church of England are included, as are lists of local and personal Acts for the year. There is a noticeable delay in publishing, which the Stationery Office is working at reducing.

For early statutes

Statutes at Large

Most well known edition by Owen Ruffhead and revised by Charles Runnington. This covers early statutes from the Magna Carta 1215 to 1785. Available on microfilm.

Statutes of the Realm

Published by the Record Commissioners between 1810 and 1828, these 10 volumes are another source of early statutes from 1235 to 1713. Available on microfilm.

Statutory instruments

Halsbury's Statutory Instruments. London: Butterworths.
ISBN: 0406996172 (set).

Arranged as an encyclopaedia and supported by an index, consolidated index, additional texts volume and monthly survey, this series has the full text of some statutory instruments and a summary of others, but only includes statutory instruments of general application. The monthly survey updates the main volumes and is arranged by subject and recent statutory instruments are in the additional texts volumes.

Finding tools for statutes and statutory instruments

Current Law Legislation Citators: Statute Citator, Statutory Instruments Citator. London: Sweet & Maxwell.

Covering 1947 onwards, the volumes are split by date. It has a list of abbreviations, an alphabetical table of statutes and statutory instruments and lists of statutes by date, with details of their current status. It also lists European legislation implemented by statutory instrument.

Halsbury's Statutes Citator. London: Butterworths

Annual companion to *Halsbury's Statutes.*

*Is It in Force?: A Guide to the Commencement of Statutes Passed Since …
(incorporating Statutes Not Yet in Force).* London: Butterworths.

Another very useful companion to *Halsbury's Statutes*, this is used for checking
on the commencement dates of Acts. Also has an alphabetical list of provisions
for which there is no commencement date set.

   Also on *Legislation Direct* (see p. 20).

Books and journals relevant to legislation

Bennion, Francis A.R. Statutory Interpretation: a Code (4th edn). London:
Butterworths, 2002. cci, 1,284p. ISBN: 0406943052.

Specialist work for practitioners to understand the meaning and interpretation
of legislation. It has been updated to include the implications of the Human
Rights Act 1998.

Statute Law Review. Oxford: Oxford University Press in association with the
Statute Law Society. ISSN: 0144-3593 (SLR).

Published with the Statute Law Society, this journal has articles on legislation
and the legislative process and the drafting and interpretation of statutes. Covers
primary and secondary legislation, codes of practice in Commonwealth and
other jurisdictions, European Union legislation and sometimes international law.
   Available on *LexisNexis Professional.*

Online services

These are the online services most relevant to finding legislation. In addition to
the sources listed here, specialist online services concentrating on a particular
subject often include relevant statutes and statutory instruments (see Part 2).

Lawtel (see p. 34)

Has United Kingdom and European Union legislation.

Legislation Direct (*http://www.lexisnexis.co.uk/site/Legislation-Direct.asp*)

Part of *Butterworths LexisNexis Direct Services*, this has the full amended text of statutes and statutory instruments. Includes *Is It in Force?* and Bill tracker databases.

LexisNexis Professional (see p. 34)

Has full coverage of United Kingdom and European Union legislation.

New Law Online (see p. 35)

The current awareness service has legislation.

UK Statutes and *UK Statutory Instruments* (*The Justis Databases* (see p. 33))

Westlaw UK (see p. 35)

Full text of United Kingdom and European Union legislation.

Websites

Acts of the UK Parliament (*http://www.hmso.gov.uk/acts.htm*)

Her Majesty's Stationery Office site has the full text of Public General Acts since 1988, Local Acts from 1991 and statutory instruments since 1987. Statutes for Scotland, Wales and Northern Ireland are included as well as those for the United Kingdom. The aim is to publish on the site simultaneously with the print version or at least only 24 hours behind. The statutes and statutory instruments are published as originally passed and unannotated. Moreover, it is hard to search and find a particular section of an Act. The commercial online services, although not free, are much easier to use.

Bills (*http://www.parliament.the-stationery-office.co.uk/pa/pabills.htm*)

Part of the Parliament site, this has the full text of House of Commons and House of Lords Bills now before Parliament.

Chronological Tables of Local and Private Acts (*http://www.legislation.hmso .gov.uk/legislation/chron-tables/chron-index.htm*)

The HMSO site includes the tables authorised by the Law Commission and Scottish Law Commission covering private and personal Acts from 1539 to 2001 and local Acts from 1797 to 2001. The *Chronological Table of the Statutes* is to be included soon.

Tracing Acts of Parliament (*http://www.parliament.uk/commons/lib/fs44.pdf*)

House of Commons Library factsheet is viewable online or downloadable as an Adobe Acrobat pdf file.

Weekly Information Bulletin (*http://www.parliament.the-stationery-office.co.uk/ pa/cm/cmwib.htm*)

Has full list of Public Bills before Parliament and their progress.

Finding legislation

Bills

Most libraries do not buy individual Bills, but some are published in journals and in legal encyclopaedias. It is probably easiest to go to the Parliament website for Bills currently before Parliament (*http://www .parliament.the-stationery-office.co.uk/pa/pabills.htm*). With each Bill, there is information on its progress and any amendments listed under the Bill separately. A full set of Bills is kept in the Guildhall Library, London.

To check how far a Bill has got through Parliament, check the Bill on the Parliament website. Alternatively, look in the latest *Weekly Information Bulletin* (hardcopy or at *http://www.parliament.the-stationery-office.co.uk/pa/cm/cmwib.htm*) for information on all the current Bills. In addition, *Current Law Monthly Digest* has the heading 'Progress of Bills' and the Practitioner section of *New Law Journal* will also tell you how far Bills have got. *Hansard* has the Parliamentary debates on Bills in full. The Parliament website has *Hansard* for both the House of Commons and House of Lords.

Statutes: public general Acts

As with Bills, most libraries will not buy the individual statutes. There are the three printed sources, the official series, *Public General Acts*, and the two annotated series, *Current Law Statutes* and *Halsbury's Statutes*. All have a problem of incurring some delay in publishing, but do check the loose-leaf binders of *Current Law Statutes* and *Halsbury's Statutes* when looking for recent Acts. The HMSO site *http://www.hmso.gov.uk/acts.htm* is right up to date but is hard to use. If available, the online services *Westlaw UK* and *LexisNexis Professional* are the best sources.

As with cases, it is important to understand how statutes are cited. It is usual to give the short title of the statute (this is the title by which it is normally known), followed by the year it received royal assent and the chapter number. The latter is a running number for that year. An example is Administration of Justice Act 1985 c.61, which is the 61st statute for that year. Statutes are divided into sections and normally subsections. So, 1985 c.61, s. 40(1) refers to section 40, subsection 1 of this Act, which is concerned with the issue of legal aid.

The way citations for statutes are done are much easier than used to be the case before 1 January 1963 when a very complicated system was used. The citation did not use the calendar year and chapter number, but rather the regnal year or years of the Parliamentary session in which it was passed and chapter number, counting from the year the Monarch came to the throne. For example, the Administration of Justice (Judges and Pensions) Act 9 Eliz ch.3 was passed in 1960. It is useful to understand about regnal years because sometimes pre-1963 statutes will be wanted. Lists of regnal years are often to be found in law dictionaries.

To find statutes on a particular subject, *Halsbury's Statutes* and *Halsbury's Laws* are the best printed sources; the volumes for both are arranged by subject and they have detailed subject indexes. Otherwise, the online services can be searched by keyword and free text and you can normally restrict your search to legislation.

To check whether a statute is in force, look in the latest version of *Is It In Force?* To be completely sure, look in *Halsbury's Statutes* noter-up service for any recent change.

To see if an Act or particular section has been repealed or amended, applied or referred to, look in *Current Law Legislation Citators*.

Statutes: local and personal Acts

It is rare that these will be needed. The Guildhall Library, London does have them and they are on the HMSO site from 1991 onwards (*http://www.hmso.gov.uk/acts*).

Statutory instruments

The main printed source is *Halsbury's Statutory Instruments*, but this is not a full set. There is a subject index in the consolidated index and a list by year and statutory instrument number in the chronological list of instruments.

A full set of statutory instruments is kept at the Guildhall Library, London and the HMSO site has them from 1987, including draft statutory instruments. They are also on the online services such as *Westlaw* and *LexisNexis Professional* and often included in loose-leaf encyclopaedias.

The citation of a statutory instrument is quite straightforward, for each statutory instrument in a year has its own number, e.g. Utilities Act 2000 (Supply of Information) Regulations 2000/2956.

A particular statutory instrument can be traced in the statutory instruments citator part of *Current Law Legislation Citators*. There is an alphabetical list of statutory instruments, which can be checked for year and statutory instrument number. Then the statutory instrument can be looked up using these to see if it has been amended, applied or revoked. An alternative is *Halsbury's Statutory Instruments Citator*.

3

Secondary material

Legal journals

Journal articles should be consulted to keep up to date with the latest legal developments, which is essential, and also as a source of comment and criticism on legal topics.

A variety of law journals can be identified, with their different characteristics and uses. Academic journals contain major articles on legal topics, comments on cases and statutes and book reviews. These are published between two and six times a year. Foreign academic journals are useful for a comparative view of legal trends. Practitioner journals are usually published weekly and are more topical, with brief reports on cases, statutes and new British government initiatives and short articles on latest developments. These titles can still be of interest to students wanting to be knowledgeable about changes in the law. The final category is specialist journals, concentrating on one area of the law and they have a mixture of news and substantial articles.

The following section lists authoritative academic journals, general in scope. Some very well known foreign journals are included. Specialist journals are listed in Part 2 under the relevant subject and practitioner journals are in Chapter 5 on the legal profession.

After the list of journals, there is a section on the citation of journals and advice on tracing journal articles.

Academic journals

Cambridge Law Journal. Cambridge: Cambridge University Press. ISSN: 0008-1973 (CLJ).

Three issues a year.

Current Legal Problems. Oxford: Oxford University Press. ISSN: 0070-1998 (CLP).

Annual review, collecting together articles and lectures on a wide-range of topics, including analyses of important recent cases.

Harvard Law Review. Cambridge, MA: Harvard Law Review Association. ISSN: 0017-811X (HLR).

Respected American academic journal. Tables of contents, abstracts and occasional articles in full can be found at *http://www.harvardlawreview.org.*

The Juridical Review. Edinburgh and London: W. Green. ISSN: 0022-6785 (JR).

Law Commission. Discussion Papers and Law Commission Reports (Law Com).

The papers of the law reform body on the topics being considered for change. Also available on their website *http://www.lawcom.gov.uk* (see p. 37).

The Law Quarterly Review. London: Sweet & Maxwell. ISSN: 0023-933X (LQR).

Legal Studies: the Journal of the Society of Legal Studies. London: Butterworths. ISSN: 0261-3875 (LS).

This continues *Legal Studies: the Journal of the Society of Public Teachers of Law.*

Modern Law Review. Oxford: Blackwell. ISSN: 0026-7961 (MLR).

Six issues a year.

New Law Journal. London: Butterworths. ISSN: 0306-6479 (NLJ).

Weekly, this is a good way to keep abreast of new developments.

Available on *LexisNexis Professional.* In addition, there is a companion website *http://www.new-law-journal.co.uk*, which reviews this and next week's issue, but most features are only available by subscription. The site has a link to the free e-mailing service run by Butterworths, *Daily Update.*

Nottingham Law Journal: Journal of Nottingham Law School. Nottingham: Nottingham Law School, Nottingham Trent University. ISSN: 0965-0660 (Nott LJ).

Two issues a year. This continues *Trent Law Journal.*

Oxford Journal of Legal Studies. London: Oxford University Press on behalf of the Faculty of Law, University of Oxford. ISSN: 0143-6503 (OJLS).

Covers comparative and international law, European Union law, legal history and philosophy and interdisciplinary material relevant to law.

Available on *LexisNexis Professional.*

Scottish Law Commission. Discussion Papers, Consultation Papers and Reports.

The papers are also available on the Commission's website (*http://www .scotlawcom.gov.uk*) (see p. 37).

Yale Law Journal. New Haven, CT: Yale Law Journal. ISSN: 0044-0094 (YLJ).

American academic journal.

Electronic sources of journals

Many law journals, practitioner and specialist works among them, have made issues available through legal databases such as *Westlaw UK* and *LexisNexis Professional* and through serial services such as *Emerald* (*http://www.emerald*

-library.com), *Ingenta* (*http://www.ingenta.com/*), *JSTOR* (*http://uk.jstor.org/jstor/*), *Kluwer Online* (*http://www.kluweronline.com*) and *SwetsWise* (*http://www.swetswise.com/public/login.do*). It is well worth checking on these, although how long the run is will vary and it may be as short as a year. *LexisNexis Professional* has an impressive number of full-text British legal journals. *Westlaw* includes mainly American journals, but there are also some British examples included.

Web journals

Web Journal of Current Legal Issues (*http://webjcli.ncl.ac.uk*) ISSN: 1360-1326.

Based at the University of Newcastle upon Tyne, this web journal is published fortnightly. It focuses on current legal issues in case law, law reform, legislation, legal research, policy related socio-legal research, legal information and information technology and practice. The articles, comments, case notes, legal information and information sections are refereed.

Finding journals

Citation of journals

It should be straightforward to find a particular journal article where you have the reference, but students do seem to struggle with it, in particular not recognising what is a volume or page number. There are many ways of citing journals, unlike law reports and statutes, but the basic elements are date, volume number, journal title in full or abbreviated form and page number. A typical example of a citation is Norrie, Alan. From Criminal Law to Legal Theory: the Mysterious Case of the Reasonable Glue Sniffer. (2002) 67 MLR 538. The minimum needed to find an article is the journal name or abbreviation, date or volume number and preferably the page number.

The first source for checking citations is Raistrick, Donald. *Index to Legal Citations and Abbreviations* (2nd edn). If this does not have it, a website that might help is the *Cardiff Index to Legal Abbreviations* (*http://www.legalabbrevs.cardiff.ac.uk*). This has a database of common legal abbreviations, including law reports and law journals.

Finding articles on a particular topic

There is a choice of printed and online sources of journal references.

Printed sources

Journal's own indexes

Many of the journals, particularly academic ones, have annual indexes as well as content pages. But this is a laborious way of tracing articles unless you are sure the article is in a particular journal and have some idea of the year.

Current Law (see p. 43)

The monthly issues list articles at the end of each subject heading and the yearbooks have them at the end of the volume. Generally, only longer articles are listed by these publications, with short case notes and so on excluded. Moreover, the fairly rigid list of subject headings may mean it is hard to find what is wanted.

Halsbury's Laws of England (p. 43)

The annual abridgement to *Halsbury's Laws* has lists of articles written in the last year under each subject heading.

Electronic sources

Current Awareness for Legal Information Managers (CALim Database) (*http://ials.sas.ac.uk/library/caware/caware.htm*)

This classified list from the Institute of Advanced Legal Studies includes references to recent journal articles.

Lawtel

An online source of reference is *Lawtel*, which has summaries of articles and abstracts of articles from more than 50 specialist and general legal publications, including the legal supplements from most broadsheets. The abstracts link to cited cases and legislation. Full-text delivery of journal articles by fax is available at an extra cost and *Lawtel's Update Service* covers abstracts of articles, with weekly journals summarised very quickly.

Legal Journals Index

A very powerful way of finding references is the online version of *Legal Journals Index* (see p. 206 for the companion *European Legal Journals Index*). *Legal Journals Index* is available on *Current Legal Information* (see p. 32) and *Westlaw* and can be used to find references to articles on a particular topic or to locate an article by a particular author. You can search by subject and keyword, legislation cited, case cited, journal title, article and author. Searches can be restricted by date. Only an abstract of the article is retrieved, with enough information to identify the article and to see if it is relevant, although *Westlaw* has quite a lot of British journals in full text on their database. *Legal Journals Index* is very much more up to date than the printed sources and is very easy to search. One problem is that it may be frustrating to find interesting references to sources thrown up, particularly to specialist and practitioner works, the full text of which may not be easily available to you.

> ## *Finding journal titles*
>
> *UK Law Journals Directory (http://elj.warwick.ac.uk/juk/directory.html)*
> This is a comprehensive list of UK law journals published in electronic and
> hard-copy form, with bibliographic and contact information which may be
> useful for stock selection. The drawback is that the list was done in 1997
> and has not been updated; this means that, although it is still useful, you
> do need to check details of a journal before purchasing. The publishers of
> *UK Law Journals Directory* hope that at some point the list will be
> updated and broadened to cover global electronic law journals.

General online services

These subscription services are comprehensive, up to date and quick and easy to
use. They are usually available through the Internet, but there may also be CD-
Rom versions. They normally have a range of search options, including key words,
free text, parties, courts and judges, statute names and sections and you should be
able to e-mail your results as well as print and download to a floppy. You can
normally restrict your search to particular material, such as cases or statutes, if that
is what you want. Many databases now have an e-mail alerter service so you can
request to be sent details of developments in your area of interest.

The drawback is that all this comes at a price and the services can involve
expensive subscriptions for libraries and firms, depending on the number of
users. However, some services do have flexible subscriptions, including a daily
rate for individuals.

Butterworths LexisNexis Direct Services

A library of British law, including online versions of well-known works published
by Butterworths across a wide-range of topics. Uses an enhanced version of

NETbos to enable users to access information easily and quickly via the Internet. Among the libraries is *Scots Law Direct*, an online service for Scottish law. More information about *Direct Services* is available at *http://www.butterworths.co.uk/ butterworths.asp*. Details of the individual services are given in Part 2 and include:

All England Direct
Banking Law Direct
Case Search
Civil Procedure Online
Commercial Property Law Direct
Corporate Law Direct
Crime Online
Encyclopaedia of Forms and Precedents
Family and Child Law Direct
Insolvency Law Direct
Intellectual Property and Technology Direct
Journal of International Banking and Financial Law
Legislation Direct.

Current Legal Information (CLI)

A subscription reference service, not full-text, which is available as a CD-Rom or on the Internet. It splits into *Current Law Cases*, which is a digest of all reported cases from 1947, *Case Citator*, *Legislation Citator*, a guide to legislative developments, *LRDI*, an index of legal current awareness information, and the excellent *Legal Journals Index*, *European Legal Journals Index* and *Financial Journals Index*, abstracts of business and financial as well as law journals. CLI is a useful tool, but with so many full-text services around, it can be frustrating only to retrieve citations.

A separate service by Sweet & Maxwell but complementary to it is *DocDel*, which is an online document delivery service of over 900 legal and financial journals. Law firms might find this useful.

The Justis Databases

These databases provided by Context Limited, an independent electronic publisher, are available as a CD-Rom or web service. Though expensive, it nonetheless has an impressive scope of case and statute law and includes:

Celex
Civil Procedure Rules
Commercial Judicial Review Reports
Common Market Law Reports
Criminal Appeal Reports and Sentencing
Daily Cases
ECJ Proceedings
Electronic Irish Reports and Digest
Family Law Reports
Human Rights
Industrial Cases Reports
Law Reports Digest
Mental Health Law Reports
OJ Daily
Prison Law Reports
RAPID Database
The Times Law Reports
UK Statutes
UK Statutory Instruments
The Weekly Law Reports

Part of the service is *JustCite*, a comprehensive index to key British and European legal and official information. A useful bonus on the Justis website is the free legal news (*http://www.justis.com/news/news.html*) with links to news sites. Also worth a look is John Cooper's *Legal Focus*, with weekly articles by a barrister on current legal matters.

For more information see: *http://www.justis.com/navigate/main.html*.

Lawtel

Very useful current awareness service aimed mainly at practitioners and now owned by Sweet & Maxwell. It is updated daily. Has the full text of cases since 1980, statutes since 1987 and comprehensive coverage of Bills and command papers from 1997/1998. Full text of practice directions since 1998 are online and personal injury quantum reports are included. Abstracts of major journals are added.

Lawtel splits into:

Lawtel Civil Procedure
Lawtel EU – cases, legislation, Commission reports and articles
Lawtel Human Rights – an information service on the Human Rights Act 1998
Lawtel Local Government
Lawtel Personal Injury
Lawtel UK – case law, legislation and an articles index
Includes *Blackstone's Civil Practice Online*.

Another useful feature is the *Daily Update*, which has new cases, statutes, and bills and journals all together and is a good way of keeping right up to date with changes.

The specialist areas are not included in all the types of subscriptions to *Lawtel*. A full-text service of case transcripts and journal articles is available to professional subscribers.

For more information see: *http://www.lawtel.co.uk*.

LexisNexis Professional

A comprehensive subscription service comparable to *Westlaw* which includes the full text of cases, statutes and journals, and depending on the particular subscription, covers British, European and American law. There are a large number of British legal journals on it and the law reports include *The Times*. There are a variety of subscriptions to choose from, including fee-based systems and daily passes. The service has been recently redesigned with a new look, new navigation and a reduction in the use of legal jargon. A new current awareness form brings together current legal information, including cases from the last week, journal articles and news from the past month, and *Halsbury's Laws of England Monthly Review* in weekly and other updates. It is possible to go through from here to selected practice areas, including banking, civil procedure and employment, for browsing or searching.

For more information see: *http://www.lexisnexis.co.uk.*

A different product is *LexisNexis Executive,* which is for newspaper, business and company information.

Localaw UK

A Sweet & Maxwell legal research service for local government, covering administration, environmental law, compulsory purchase, housing, highways, planning, and landlord and tenant. There is an e-mail alerting service, with daily current awareness updates and weekly digests with analysis. Information about the service is available at *http://www.localaw.co.uk.*

New Law Online

A very up-to-date subscription current awareness service, similar to *Lawtel* in scope. The full judgment is added within 48 hours. The service is owned by Sweet & Maxwell and covers treaties and European Union material as well as British statute and case law. The database is arranged by practice areas, such as criminal law and the European Court of Justice. It is possible to search for a case by name, by court, by judge, by counsel and by solicitor. *The Alerter Service* means subscribers can be e-mailed with changes to English and European case law. *New Law Online* is an excellent way of being fully up to date with judgments from the High Court, Court of Appeal, Privy Council, House of Lords and the European Court of Justice. For more information see: *http://www.newlawonline.com.*

Westlaw UK

Very impressive and comprehensive subscription service from Sweet & Maxwell and the West Group, covering the full text of British, European Union and American cases and legislation. Covers many law reports, including many of Sweet & Maxwell's specialised series. The exact pagination from the original print version of the law report is given for citation purposes.

Westlaw UK has current awareness, journals and commentary from Sweet & Maxwell publications, including *Archbold* and *Civil Procedure (The White Book)*, as well as cases and legislation, altogether in one service.

The service includes the full text of some journals as well as having the very useful *Legal Journals Index*. There are specialist practice areas, one of them being Scottish law, including case law and Scottish legislation from Westminster and Holyrood. There is also a separate *Scots Law Legal Journals Index*. Westlaw is updated three times a day.

Westlaw UK offers a range of alternative subscriptions and it might suit law firms to pick out certain practice areas, such as landlord and tenant or civil procedure, and just subscribe to those.

For more information see: *http://www.westlaw.co.uk*.

General websites

Amid all the dross of the web, there are government and other free sites that are authoritative and worth looking at. The official sites of public bodies and departments can be a wealth of information and there are also some very useful sites run by solicitors and universities. These may have information on the law or be gateways, providing structured guides to global legal information, or portals with current information as well as links to sites. Most of the sites are free and where registration or a fee is required, this is indicated in the section below. Some sites have a mixture of free and closed access areas, which have more detailed information.

The following list is split into official sites and authoritative independent sites, gateways and portals which can be recommended. Some solicitor sites are included, as are some campaigning organisations, and they both can be very useful, but it is worth remembering that they may be concerned to promote themselves. Those sites covering a particular topic or aspect of the law are listed with that subject in Part 2. There is also an index at the back of the book listing all the websites mentioned.

Official sites

Her Majesty's Stationery Office (*http://www.hmso.gov.uk*)

In particular, the Legislation Section is useful for the full texts of statutes and statutory instruments. The site is to be relaunched as *HMSOnline.*

Law Commission (*http://www.lawcom.gov.uk*)

Has a list of all its reports, but more importantly has the full text of reports since 1995 and consultation papers since 1996 available for downloading using Adobe Acrobat. The Commission's annual reports are also on the site.

The Official Documents Web Site (*http://www.official-documents.co.uk*)

Run by TSO (The Stationery Office), this site has some British government papers, including House of Commons papers, command papers and departmental papers on a range of topics. The documents are split by date into 1994–2001 and 2002 onwards. The site does not have Acts of Parliament or statutory instruments. If you cannot locate a government paper here, try the site for the individual department.

Scottish Law Commission (*http://www.scotlawcom.gov.uk*)

Includes pdf files of all discussion papers and reports since September 2000 and some earlier ones are being added.

UK Online.gov.uk (*http://www.ukonline.gov.uk*)

This is the first call for finding public information on the Internet, with a search engine covering 1.5 million web pages of departments and official bodies. The site also carries British government news.

United Kingdom Parliament (*http://www.parliament.uk*)

Has an abundance of information about Parliament and, in particular, gives access to Hansard, the text of Bills before Parliament and House of Lords judgments.

Independent sites

BAILII (British and Irish Legal Information Institute) (*http://www.bailii.org*)

This is a new free site developed by cooperation between the Australian Legal Information Institute (AUSTLII) and bodies in Britain. It covers legislation and cases from 1996 onwards, including English, Scottish, Irish and Northern Ireland law. The data on the site is taken from several sources, including CD-Roms, courts and government departments as well as the web, and is converted into a common format. There are also links to other jurisdictions at the World Legal Information Institute site (*http://www.worldlii.org*). BAILII has an additional role in advocating the use of neutral citations.

BOPCAS: British Official Publications Current Awareness Service (*http://www .bopcas.soton.ac.uk*)

This is a subscription site, with registered users being able to search and browse over 26,000 references to key British official publications from July 1995 onwards.

CataLaw: Catalogue of Worldwide Links of Law and Government Sites (*http:// www.catalaw.com*)

Allows searches for sites by region and by topic, covering international law and British law.

ConnectingLegal (*http://www.connectinglegal.com*)

The site for legal directory information and other resources run by Waterlows caters for the public, students and lawyers. There are searchable directories, links to other online legal sources, recent legal news, a book search and access to the Central Law Training Course database.

Consilio (*http://www.spr-consilio.com*)

This site owned by Semple Piggot Rochez Internet Law School (see p. 51) includes a wealth of legal material, although the frames and general clutter make it hard to use. There is the choice of limited access if you do not register, free membership for more access and a subscription for further materials. The site includes articles, lecture notes, case notes and recorded lectures. Has pdf files, audio and video.

Elexica (*http://www.elexica.com*)

There is free registration for this online legal resource run by the firm Simmons & Simmons. Has updates arranged by topic, a European Union diary and links to other sites.

Freelawyer (*http://www.freelawyer.co.uk*)

Run by Judicium Limited, this site has information for people with a legal problem. There is a list of topics, such as driving, and a summary of the law, which people can look at before deciding whether to pay to speak to a solicitor.

Global-Law.net (*http://www.global-law.net*)

This legal search engine is split into different categories, including subject area, solicitors, barristers, articles, case law, books and magazines, and covers British and European Union law and American law.

Institute of Advanced Legal Studies (IALS) (*http://ials.sas.ac.uk*)

The Institute's site has three useful resources. The first is *eagle-i,* which has links to independently maintained websites arranged by topic, by country and by international organisations. There is a list of electronic discussion lists, as well as links to the IALS Library catalogue and list of serials (see p. 64). Another service is *Current Awareness for Legal Information Managers (CALim Database),* which is a classified list of newly published books and journal articles (see p. 64). The final service is the new *Current Legal Research Topic Database Project,* listing current postgraduate legal research (see p. 50).

Jurist UK: The Legal Education Network (*http://jurist.law.cam.ac.uk*)

This is the British-based version of the non-commercial forum for law professors, lawyers, judges, students, journalists and the public to share a wide range of legal information and ideas. The site has news and research and using the law locator it is possible to search for cases, bills, statutes and statutory instruments. There are links to government and parliamentary sites, legal research tools and to major online services for which passwords are needed. There is also an A–Z list of links to academic law pages run by professors. These sites have a variety of reading lists, scholarly publications and links on them. Finally, the American, Canadian and Australian Jurist sites can be reached from the British site.

Law Lists Info (*http://www.lib.uchicago.edu/~llou/lawlists/info.html*)

This is a site to foster networking, legal research and exchange and dissemination of legal information worldwide. It includes electronic discussion groups run by mailing list management software and law-related Usenet newsgroups.

Law on the Web: The UK Public's Favourite Gateway to Legal Information (*http://www.lawontheweb.co.uk*)

Run by Martin Davies, this site has the law on particular areas, with references to relevant books. It is possible to search for a law firm and there is a follow-up charged service providing advice by phone. It has a sister site *Can I Claim?: The Accident Compensation Site* (*http://www.caniclaim.com*) (see p. 151).

Lawlinks (*http://library.ukc.ac.uk/library/lawlinks*)

Excellent site run by Sarah Carter at the University of Kent at Canterbury with an annotated list of websites covering gateways and portals, British resources and government sites and news, special legal topics, other jurisdictions, international law, human rights and private international law. The legal profession, publishers and general resources including discussion lists for law are also included, as is a list of legal abbreviations based on the holdings of the University's Templeman Library.

Lawzone: The Online Law Community (*http://www.lawzone.co.uk*)

A slightly cluttered but improving and developing site which is aimed at providing information, news, resources and tools to lawyers. Has links to other websites. Unusually, the site also provides light relief, with humour, including a law joke of the week.

Legal Resources in the UK and Ireland (maintained by Delia Venables) (*http://www.venables.co.uk*)

Excellent independent site with links to useful legal resources. It is split into information for individuals, lawyers, companies and students, including course and career information.

Scottish Law Online (*http://www.scottishlaw.org.uk*)

This very detailed and impressive independently run web portal for Scottish law has an A–Z of the law, with links to relevant sites. The site covers law firm directories, courts, legislation, government bodies, societies and professional bodies and universities.

SOSIG (Social Science Information Gateway) (*http://www.sosig.ac.uk/law/*)

The law section of the Social Science Information Gateway, edited by experts from IALS and the University of Bristol Law Library, comments on and gives access to legal information resources on the Internet. It evaluates sites offering primary and secondary materials for British and European Union law, international law, other jurisdictions and law by subject area. This is an excellent way to look for relevant sites, both official and privately run.

Swarb.co.uk (*http://www.swarb.co.uk*)

Mainly by David Swarbrick, this is an impressive online source of British law, featuring *Lawbytes* and *Cases Lawindex*. The *Lawbytes* consist of about 400 short notes on legal topics, aimed at clients rather than practitioners. There is a summary of case law, with links to the full text provided by Lawindexpro. There are also extracts of various Acts and Conventions, with external links to the HMSO site. Another useful tool is *Cases Lawindex*, which covers case law, with a selection from the subscription service provided by Lawindexpro. The case index has references to all cases in *The Times* and the legal update section of the Law Society's *Gazette* from January 1992. The index also covers reports from *The Independent* from 1993 to 1996.

UK250 Legal Websites (*http://www.uk250.co.uk/legal*)

This is part of the UK250 web guide to UK sites arranged by subject. The law section has a couple of pages of links, including a featured legal website of the day, and has links to related pages on legal advice, solicitors and police.

Wales Legislation Online (*http://www.wales-legislation.org.uk*)

Managed by Cardiff Law School, this site has an explanation of the functions of the Assembly and the text of the secondary legislation made by them, arranged by subject.

Finding tools and law dictionaries

This section includes citation books, major works for finding the law on a particular subject and law dictionaries.

Checking legal abbreviations

A common question at the law enquiry desk is what a citation stands for. The best tool is Raistrick, Donald. *Index to Legal Citations and Abbreviations* (2nd edn). London: Bowker Saur, 1993. 497p. ISBN: 185739061X. Ten years old, this is still indispensable for checking abbreviations and a copy should be on all enquiry desks. However, you will have to look at other tools for more recent abbreviations. Those listed in *Current Law Year Book* and *Current Law Case Citator* are useful, although neither is nearly as comprehensive.

The book by French, Derek. *How to Cite Legal Authorities*. London: Blackstone Press, 1996. 284p. ISBN: 1854313150 has a dictionary of abbreviations for law reports and journals and explains the elements of citations for cases, statutes, secondary legislation and journals. This book is principally for people who need to know how to cite correctly in written work. Because it is a few years old, it does not cover neutral citations. A website that might help is the *Cardiff Index to legal Abbreviations* (*http://www.legalabbrevs.cardiff.ac.uk*). From Cardiff University Information Services, this has common legal abbreviations, including law reports and journals.

Finding material by subject

Printed sources

These printed sources are well-established and comprehensive tools and it is worth knowing about them.

Current Law Monthly Digest. London: Sweet & Maxwell. ISSN: 0968-3194.

A way of tracking down recent developments, particularly in case law. The latest issue cumulates what has happened so far in the year. It is superseded by *Current Law Year Book.*

Current Law Year Book. London: Sweet & Maxwell (CLYB).

The subject index refers you to an abstract. There is also a case index and there are some references to journal articles. Useful start to research, although you do also need to check the *Current Law Monthly Digest* to keep up with changes.

The Digest (see p. 9)

Halsbury's Laws of England. ISBN: 0406047766 (set).

Major reference tool. Search by topic or by case for comment and references to the relevant sources. Need to check in loose-leaf volumes for any changes since the bound volumes. There is a monthly review for very recent developments.

   Halsbury's Laws is also available online on *LexisNexis* and as part of *Butterworths LexisNexis Direct Services* as *Halsbury's Law Direct*, which has the current 50 volumes and the combined text of the latest cumulative supplement and noter-up issue.

Online services

An alternative to the printed sources are the online services, if available; one search may find all you need, you may be able to get the full text and you won't be hampered by a particular issue or volume being missing. There is also less delay in publishing, so the information is more up to date.

All the general online services are searchable by subject (see p. 31). Particularly useful are the current awareness services such as *Lawtel* and *New Law Online*.

Legal Updater
Reference tool and part of *Butterworths LexisNexis Direct Services*.

Law dictionaries

Law dictionaries with succinct legal definitions are useful for students. It is also a good idea to have English language dictionaries available in the law library and in easy reach.

Books

Bone, Sheila. *Osborn's Concise Law Dictionary* (9th edn). London: Sweet & Maxwell, 2001. vii, 466p. ISBN: 0421753404.

Burke, John (ed.). *Jowitt's Dictionary of English Law*. London: Sweet & Maxwell, 1977. 2v. ISBN: 0421230908.

The classic law dictionary has been kept up to date by cumulative supplements.

Butterworths Glossary of Scottish and European Legal Terms (2nd edn). London: Butterworths, 2002. 1v. ISBN: 0406949476.

Collin, P.H. *Dictionary of Law* (3rd edn). Teddington: Collins Publishing, 2002. 398p. ISBN: 1901659437.

A CD-Rom version is also available and the dictionary can be searched online at the website *ConnectingLegal* (*http://www.connectinglegal.com*, see p. 38); you look for particular legal terms rather than browsing, and there are over 7,500 searchable terms.

Hoof, D.C. van, Vebruggen, D. and Stoll, C.H. *Elsevier's Legal Dictionary in English, German, French, Dutch and Spanish*. Amsterdam: London: Elsevier Science, 2001. ix, 1,420p. ISBN: 0444817859.

James, John S. *Stroud's Judicial Dictionary of Words and Phrases* (5th edn). London: Sweet & Maxwell, 1986. 6v. ISBN: 0421366303.

Authoritative work, kept up to date by cumulative supplements.

Martin, Elizabeth A. (ed.). *A Dictionary of Law* (Oxford Paperback Reference). Oxford: Oxford University Press, 2002. 551p. ISBN: 0198603991.

Spine title: *Oxford Dictionary of Law.*

Murdoch, Henry. *Murdoch's Dictionary of Irish Law: A Sourcebook* (rev. 3rd edn). Dublin: Topaz Publications, 2000. xii, 896p. ISBN: 0951403257.

Previous edn: *A Dictionary of Irish Law.* 1993.

Penner, J.E. *Mozley and Whiteley's Law Dictionary* (12th edn). London: Butterworths, 2001. 391p. ISBN: 0406913587.

Trayner, Lord, John. *Trayner's Latin Maxims Collected from the Institutional Writers on the Law of Scotland and Other Sources* (4th edn). Edinburgh: W. Green, 1993. xvi, 635p. ISBN: 0414010612.

Vasan, R.S. (editor-in-chief). *Latin Words and Phrase for Lawyers.* Don Mills, Ont.: Datinder S. Sodhi for Law and Business Publications, 1980. 335p. ISBN: 0889290040.

Walker, David M. *The Oxford Companion to Law.* Oxford: Clarendon Press, 1980. ix, 1,366p. ISBN: 019866110X.

An encyclopaedia of Western law.

Web-based law dictionaries

Collin, P.H. *Dictionary of Law* (3rd edn) at **ConnectingLegal** (*http://www .connectinglegal.com*)

Duhaime's Law Dictionary (*http://www.duhaime.org/dictionary/diction.htm*)
An alternative to the printed dictionaries is this online version.

Law Dictionaries.Com (*http://www.lawdictionaries.com*)

Has a range of dictionaries and other tools searchable online, not just general items, including *Duhaime's Law Dictionary*, but also specialist items for legal Latin, commercial law, crime, human rights, family law and international law. It is also possible to buy printed versions at this site.

4

Legal research, using law libraries, law librarianship and teaching law

Books

Bradney, Anthony et al. *How to Study Law* (4th edn). London: Sweet & Maxwell, 2000. ix, 231p. ISBN: 0421717203.

Bruce, Richard H. *Success in Law* (5th edn). London: John Murray, 2001. vi, 520p. ISBN: 0719572118.

Chatterjee, Charles. *Methods of Research in Law* (2nd edn). London: Old Bailey Press, 2000. 84p. ISBN: 1858363861.

Clinch, Peter. *Legal Information: What It Is and Where to Find It* (2nd edn). London: Aslib, 2000. 122p. ISBN: 0851424457.

Clinch, Peter. *Using a Law Library: A Student's Guide to Legal Research Skills* (2nd edn). London: Blackstone Press, 2001. xii, 346p. ISBN: 1841740292.

Researching law, including the devolved law of Wales and Scotland. David Hart contributes the guide to Scottish materials. Describes print sources, CD-Roms and the Internet.

Fothergill, Pauline (ed.). *Directory of British and Irish Law Libraries* (7th edn). Hebden Bridge: Legal Information Resources for the British and Irish Association of Law Librarians, 2002. 1v. ISBN: 1870369157.

Excellent source, with an alphabetical list of 500 law libraries or libraries with significant collections of legal material. Also has indexes by name of organisation and organisation type, with brief descriptions of special collections and the terms of admission to the libraries.

Hanson, Sharon. *Legal Method.* London: Cavendish, 1999. viii, 357p. ISBN: 1859414249.

Good introduction to the complexities of legal method, showing how to start to construct arguments.

New edition due (see publisher's site for details: *http://www.cavendish publishing.com*).

Holborn, Guy. *Butterworths Legal Research Guide* (2nd edn). London: Butterworths, 2001. xv, 423p. ISBN: 0406930236.

Comprehensive account of legal research. Updated to include electronic and Internet services.

Holmes, Nick and Venables, Delia. *Researching the Legal Web: A Guide to Legal Resources on the Internet.* London: Butterworths, 1999. 219p. ISBN: 0406921806.

A good, if somewhat dated, overview of legal material available on the Internet. The book generally has a British slant and there are comments on the sites mentioned.

Lawrence, Penny. *Law on the Internet: A Practical Guide.* London: Sweet & Maxwell, 2000. 227p. ISBN: 0421737808.

McLeod, T.I.T. *Legal Method* (4th edn, Palgrave Law Masters). Basingstoke: Palgrave Macmillan, 2002. xxviii, 345p. ISBN: 033397025X.

Popular with students.

Roznovschi, Mirela. *Toward a Cyberlegal Culture.* Ardsley, NJ: Transnational, 2001. xvii, 230p. ISBN: 1571051686.

Sets out the general principles for successful searching.

Thomas, Philip. *Learning about Law Lecturing* (Teaching and Learning Manuals). Coventry: National Centre for Legal Education, University of Warwick, 2000. ISBN: 1902730062.

Thomas, Philip and Knowles, John. *Dane and Thomas: How to Use a Law Library* (4th edn). London: Sweet & Maxwell, 2001. xviii, 294p. ISBN: 0421744103.

Legal research including using the library and the library catalogue. Previous edition published as: *How to Use a Law Library.* 1998.

Williams, Glanville. *Glanville Williams: Learning the Law* (12th edn). London: Sweet & Maxwell, 2002. 284p. ISBN: 0421744200.

Covers techniques for studying law.

Journals

Journal of Commonwealth Law and Legal Education. London: Cavendish. ISSN: 1476-0401 (JCLLE).

The two issues a year have information relevant to law and to legal education in the Commonwealth.

The Law Teacher: Journal of the Association of Law Teachers. London: Sweet & Maxwell. ISSN: 0303-9400.

Journal for law lecturers.

Legal Information Management: Journal of the British and Irish Association of Law Librarians. London: Sweet & Maxwell. ISSN: 1472-6696.

A must for law librarians in academic libraries or working for law firms, this replaces the *Law Librarian.* BIALL's website (*http://www.biall.org.uk* – see p. 50) has lists of contents and the occasional article in full to download.

Student Law Review. London: Cavendish. ISSN: 0961-0391.

This has short notes on all the main legal topics, including case notes, and is a handy study guide with examination topics highlighted. There are three issues a year.

Websites

Association of Law Teachers (ALT) (*http://www.lawteacher.ac.uk*)

Has links to relevant British government and educational sites, a useful list of acronyms relating to education and the *ALT Bulletin*. The latter is published on the web twice a year and has news and views on current issues of legal education and details of conferences.

BIALL (British and Irish Association of Law Librarians) (*http://www.biall .org.uk*)

Includes information about the main organisation for law librarians and has links to websites arranged by cases, legislation, legal resources and practice areas.

Current Legal Research Topic Database Project (CLRT Database) (*http://ials .sas.ac.uk/library/clrt/clrt.htm*)

Planned to be updated annually, this is a new project from IALS and is an online version of *The List of Current Legal Research Topics*, last published in 1988. The aim is to provide postgraduate students with a comprehensive listing of legal research topics being done in British law schools at PhD or MPhil level. The database is searchable by student's name, university, subject keywords, name of jurisdiction or word or words from the title of the research project.

e-lawstudent.com (*http://www.e-lawstudent.com*)

Part of *Law on the Web* (see p. 40), this is the site for the provider of online legal materials, both CD-Rom and Internet. It supports the AS and A2 law programme according to the AQA and OCR syllabi and, a recent addition, the LL B degree course.

English Law (*http://libwww.essex.ac.uk/LAW/englawguide.html*)

Prepared by Albert Sloman Library, University of Essex, this site has details of sources of materials useful to undergraduates and guidance on finding cases, statutes and journal articles.

Lawyer 2B (*http://www.lawyer2B.co.uk*)

From the Lawyer Group, this new magazine for law students has news, articles, careers and recruitment information and an online community for students, *The Common Room*.

Lex on the Net: the Website for the Lawyers of the Future (*http://www .lexonthenet.co.uk*)

Run by Legalease, this rebuilt site for students has news, links to the Bar site and law courses. Has a training contract search so students can search for suitable law firms to do their articles.

Semple Piggot Rochez Internet Law School (*http://www.spr-law.com*)

The site is for promoting the school, which is the founder of the online law degree programme for the LL B course at the University of London, as the leading provider of Internet-supported law training programmes. But the site is still very useful for law students generally, with links to current information, an online study guide and the online legal magazine *Consilio*, which is owned by the school (see p. 38).

The Society of Legal Studies (*http://www.legalscholars.ac.uk/text/index.cfm*)

The site for the SLS, the learned society of university lawyers and formerly the Society of Public Teachers of Law, is text only at the moment and still in development.

5

Information on the legal profession

This chapter covers material relevant to choosing a career as a lawyer, e.g. finding out about the profession and tracking down a law firm, and to managing law firms.

Books

Legal directories/law as a career

Bar Directory. London: Sweet & Maxwell with the General Council of the Bar.

Official annual directory of barristers' chambers. There is an online version available on the Bar Council's site (see p. 57)

Butterworths Law Directory: a Guide of Solicitors and Barristers in Private Practice, Commerce, Local Government and Public Authorities in England and Wales, Northern Ireland and Scotland. London: Martin-Hubbell in association with Butterworths.

Annual directory, including overseas firms and legal executives.

Chambers Guide to the Legal Profession. London: Chambers.

Annual with solicitors and barristers listed.

Laver, Nicola. *Blackstone's Guide to Becoming a Solicitor.* London: Blackstone Press, 2000. x, 114p. ISBN: 1841741221.

The Law Society Directory of Expert Witnesses. London: Sweet & Maxwell with the Law Society.

Useful regular publication listing corporate and individual expert witnesses in the United Kingdom and Northern Ireland. Has alphabetical list and subject index.

The Law Society of Scotland Directory of Expert Witnesses. Edinburgh: W. Green with the Law Society of Scotland.

The Scottish equivalent, covering witnesses living or willing to work in Scotland.

The Law Society's Directory of Solicitors and Barristers. London: Law Society.

The official annual guide to solicitors in England and Wales also covers legal executives and barristers.

Pritchard, John (ed.-in-chief). *The Legal 500: The Clients' Guide to the UK Legal Profession.* London: Legalease.

Published annually, with an online version of Legal 500 services at *http://www.legal500.com* (see p. 58). Useful for the editorial comment on firms.

Prospects Focus on Law (Prospects Focus Series). Manchester: CSU [for] the Law Society.

Annual career guide.

Waterlow's Solicitors' and Barristers' Directory. London: Waterlow.

Annual publication covers solicitors, barristers and education bodies. The directory can be bought with or without the diary. There is an online version at *ConnectingLegal* (*http://www.connectinglegal.com*) (see p. 38).

Office background information

The following covers material relevant to working in a law firm.

Bawdon, Fiona, Napier, Michael and Wignall, Gordon. *Conditional Fees: A Survival Guide*. London: Law Society, 2001. xx, 346p. ISBN: 1853284726.

Bouttal, Trevor and Blackburn, Bill. *Solicitor's Guide to Good Management: Checklists for Lawyers* (2nd edn). London: Law Society, 2001. 198p. ISBN: 1853287326.

Campbell, Ian. *What Every Good Lawyer Should Know*. Chalford: Management Books, 2000. 129p. ISBN: 1852523174.

Covers managing a solicitor's office.

Chandler, Roy A. and Loosemore, John. *Accounting for Success: Making Sense of Solicitor's Accounts for LPC Students, Practitioners and Law Firm Cashiers* (3rd edn). London: Butterworths, 2002. xiii, 183p. ISBN: 040695299X.

Cordery, Arthur. *Cordery on Solicitors* (9th edn). London: Butterworths. Loose-leaf. ISBN: 0406035105.

Moore, Matthew. *Quality Management for Law Firms*. London: Law Society, 2001. xix, 296p. ISBN: 1853287156.

Terrett, Andrew. *The Internet: Business Strategies for Law Firms*. London: Law Society, 2000. 224p. ISBN: 185328582X.

Journals

The following are journals for practitioners, often by the professional bodies.

BSD: Busy Solicitors' Digest. London: Longman. ISSN: 0263-4430.
Useful quick guide to latest developments.

Counsel: The Journal of the Bar of England and Wales. London: Butterworths on behalf of the General Council of the Bar.

Incorporates *Bar News*.

Gazette. London: Law Society. ISSN: 0262-1495.

The journal of the Law Society. Every fourth one is called the *Guardian*. As well as the professional news, the legal update section is worth looking at, with entries of cases which will appear in *The Weekly Law Reports* and summaries of cases in *Estates Gazette*.

Available on *LexisNexis Professional*. There is also a supporting website, *Law Gazette.co.uk* (*http://www.lawgazette.co.uk*), which has legal news and the *Gazette*'s law reports. It is possible to personalise the site to get selected information when you log on.

Journal of the Law Society of Scotland. Edinburgh: Law Society of Scotland. ISSN: 0458-8711.

Available on *LexisNexis Professional*.

The Lawyer. London: Centaur Communications. ISSN: 0953-7902.

For news about law firms and developments affecting the profession. Available on *LexisNexis Professional*.

The magazine has its own website at *http://www.thelawyer.com* (see p. 58).

The Legal Executive. London: Butterworths [for] the Institute of Legal Executives. ISSN: 0024-0362.

Solicitors Journal. London: Sweet & Maxwell. ISSN: 0038-1047 (SJ).

Online services

Lawtel

Includes *Haver's Directory of Barristers* and the *Law Firm Directory*.

Websites

Information about the legal profession can be found from the websites run by the professional bodies.

Bar Council (*www.barcouncil.org.uk*)

Has news and policy, rules and guidance, and information about barristers and how to instruct one. The site also has a link to an online version of the *Bar Directory* (*http://www.smlawpub.co.uk/online/bardirectory/login/login.cfm*). This is a joint venture between the General Council of the Bar and Sweet & Maxwell and it is based on certain sections of the directory, so while it includes chambers, practising barristers and individual barristers in employment, it does not include non-practising barristers or individuals overseas. There is free registration.

ConnectingLegal (*http://www.connectinglegal.com*) (see p. 38).

This is run by Waterlow and allows searching of their directories online, with professional, student and public versions.

Institute of Legal Executives (ILEX) (*http://www.ilex.org.uk*)

As well as having information about the Institute, its exams and professional issues, there are legislative updates, with brief information about new law and how to find out more.

Law Society (*http://www.lawsociety.org.uk*)

Has news, the Society's annual report, a link to the library and responses by the Society to legislation by topic. It also has *The Guide Online*, the online version of *The Guide to the Professional Conduct of Solicitors* (*http://www.guide-on -line.lawsociety.org.uk*) and *Solicitors Online* (*http://www.solicitors-online.com*). The latter allows you to search for solicitors by location or by name of firm or individual. There are links through to firms' websites.

Law Society of Scotland (*http://www.lawscot.org.uk*)

Similarly, this site has codes of conduct, annual reports and news. It also has a service called *Dial-a-Law*, which allows you to search by legal topic and find a solicitor who deals with problems in that area. This is backed up by a phone service.

The Lawyer (*http://www.thelawyer.com*)

The website for the legal magazine is messy and cramped, but is a source for news, stories and advertising relating to the profession. There is a free e-mail service for job vacancies, news and events.

Legal 500.com: The Official Site of the Legal 500 Series (*http://www .legal500.com*)

The site of legal publisher Legalease in conjunction with the International Centre for Commercial Law includes law firm news and the online version of *Legal 500*; it is possible to search for law firms in 70 countries, pulling up recommendations, independent editorials and directories of firms. This excellent site also covers commercial legal developments across a range of countries, with articles on specialist practice areas available in pdf.

Legal Resources in the UK and Ireland (*http://www.venables.co.uk*) (see p. 41).

Delia Venables has links to British and Irish firms on her site

Prospects.ac.uk: The UK's Official Graduate Careers Website (*http://www .prospects.ac.uk*)

The law section has useful advice on the different career options for law students.

Roll on Friday (*http://www.rollonfriday.co.uk*)

Run by former City lawyers, the site has news, views and gossip on the legal profession, including restaurant reviews and salary and other information on the top firms. Has help with searching for a job, including *Make Me an Offer*, which lets you submit your details to the site which are given to the firms anonymously, with the site acting as an intermediary.

The Trainee Solicitors' Group (*http://www.tsg.org.uk*)

There is free registration for this underdeveloped site, which has information about the group and events and the online version of the journal *The Trainee*.

Part 2

Topics

6

Introduction

Part 2 focuses on the main legal subjects, listing up-to-date and authoritative textbooks along with relevant online services and official and non-official websites, all of which might be useful to ensuring current and complete research. A general point is to make sure that it is the latest edition of a work that is being used and it is a good idea to check the publication date in the book. In law, older editions are not worth using, unless the research is from a historical point of view. Some books are updated by supplements and these should be checked too. Increasingly, books have a companion website, maintained by the author or publisher, which has more recent information or accompanying material too bulky for the book. These companion sites often link to other relevant sites and are worth looking out for. LexisNexis Butterworths Tolley (*http://www.butterworths.co.uk*, *http://www.lexisnexis .co.uk* – for publisher details see p. 218) and Cavendish (*http://www.cavendish publishing.com* – for publisher details see p. 213) have been particularly good at supporting their most popular books this way. Generally, it is a good idea to visit publishers' sites to see what information is available, whether or not you own a particular book.

An alternative to buying the hard-copy of a textbook is to purchase it in e-book form if available. Generally, e-books are cheaper and it is often possible to buy just a section rather than the whole book. Adobe Acrobat means that the book is presented in the same layout as the printed version. Cavendish have made all their textbooks and revision guides available as e-books and have details and guidance on their use on their site.

If you want to check for more material by subject than listed here, one source is the bibliography, Raistrick, Donald. *Lawyer's Law Books: A Practical Index to Legal Literature* (3rd edn). London: Bowker Saur, 1997. xxxiv, 723p. ISBN: 1857390873. It is very out of date, but it is still a good way of identifying the classic works provided you check for later editions. A newer source is *Current Awareness for Legal Information Managers (CALim Database)*, which is a classified list of newly published books and journal articles. Run by IALS library staff, this is found at *http://ials.sas.ac.uk/library/caware/caware.htm*. The list is also printed in the journal *Legal Information Management: Journal of the British and Irish Association of Law Librarians*. The online bookshops are listed in the Appendix on legal publishers and Internet bookshops.

For websites on a particular topic, *IALS eagle-i service (http://ials.sas.ac.uk/links/eagle-i.htm)* is a good start, covering British and international law. Another recommended source is Delia Venables' site *Legal Resources in the UK and Ireland (http://www.venables.co.uk)* (see p. 41). The other gateways and portals listed in Chapter 3 on general websites are also useful (see p. 36).

The remaining chapters in this part are generally arranged as follows:

- books;
- law reports;
- journals;
- online services;
- websites.

7

The law, legal history and the legal system

This chapter covers general introductions to the law and the legal system, legal theory and legal history.

The legal system has seen major changes in recent years. Examples are the Access to Justice Act 1999 establishing the Legal Services Commission and the Community Legal Service, the 1998 Civil Procedure Rules, the Human Rights Act 1998 and the Auld Committee review of criminal justice.

Books

Bailey, S.H., Gunn, Michael and Ormerod, D.C. *Smith, Bailey and Gunn on the Modern English Legal System* (4th edn). London: Sweet & Maxwell, 2002. 1,520p. ISBN: 0421741309.

Baker, J.H. *An Introduction to English Legal History* (4th edn). London: Butterworths, 2002. 600p. ISBN: 0406930538.

Barker, D.L. and Padfield, C.F. *Law* (11th edn). Oxford: Made Simple, 2002. 404p. ISBN: 0750654058.

Berlins, Marcel and Dyer, Clare. *The Law Machine* (4th edn, Penguin Law). Harmondsworth: Penguin, 1994. 200p. ISBN: 0140234780.

Coleman, Jules and Shapiro, Scott (eds). *The Oxford Handbook of Jurisprudence and Philosophy of Law*. Oxford: Oxford University Press, 2002. x, 1,050p. ISBN: 0198298242.

Derbyshire, Penny. *Eddey and Derbyshire on the English Legal System* (7th edn). London: Sweet & Maxwell, 2001. xxx, 381p. ISBN: 0421750707.

Update of *Eddey on the English Legal System*. 1996. Covers the Human Rights Act 1998 and the changes to the way judicial appointments are done.

Elliott, Catherine and Quinn, Frances. *English Legal System* (4th edn). Harlow: Longman, 2002. xxxi, 612p. ISBN: 0582473136.

Evans, Judith (ed.). *English and European Legal Systems: Textbook* (2nd edn). London: Old Bailey Press, 2001. xxvi, 389p. ISBN: 1858364051.

Farley, Jeremy. *Understanding and Using the British Legal System* (Key Advice Guides). London: Key Advice Guides, 2002. 207p. ISBN: 1900694867.

Freeman, M.D.A. *Lloyd's Introduction to Jurisprudence* (7th edn). London: Sweet & Maxwell, 2001. xl, 1,526p. ISBN: 0421690208.

With text and extracts from authoritative sources, this covers the theories of the different schools of jurisprudence from the ancient Greeks to postmodernists.

Hart, F.L.A. *The Concept of Law* (2nd edn). Oxford: Oxford University Press, 1994. xii, 315p. ISBN: 0198761228.

Keenan, Denis. *Smith and Keenan's English Law* (13th edn). Harlow: Longman, 2001. xliv, 884p. ISBN: 0582438160.

McLeod, T.I.T. *Legal Theory* (2nd edn, Palgrave Law Masters). Basingstoke: Palgrave Macmillan, 2003. 208p. ISBN: 1403904596.

Marshall, Enid A. *General Principles of Scots Law* (7th edn). Edinburgh: W. Green, 1999. xxiii, 492p. ISBN: 0414012879.

Martin, Jacqueline. *The English Legal System* (3rd edn). London: Hodder & Stoughton, 2002. xv, 298p. ISBN: 0340848545.

Paterson, A.A., Bates, T. St J.N. and Poustie, Mark R. *The Legal System of Scotland: Cases and Materials* (4th edn). Edinburgh: W. Green, 1999. xl, 483p. ISBN: 0414012739.

Richardson, Janice and Sandland, Ralph (eds). *Feminist Perspectives on Law and Theory.* London: Cavendish, 2000. xvii, 250p. ISBN: 1859415288.

Riddall, J.G. *Jurisprudence* (2nd edn). London: Butterworths, 1999. xi, 355p. ISBN: 0406900108.

Rivlin, Geoffrey. *First Steps in the Law* (2nd edn). Oxford: Oxford University Press, 2002. xi, 390p. ISBN: 0199254796.

Describes how laws are made and cases tried. Covers the administration of justice, the development of common law, the constitution, legal proof and courts.

Simmonds, N.E. *Central Issues in Jurisprudence* (2nd edn). London: Sweet & Maxwell, 2002. x, 316p. ISBN: 0421741201.

Introduction to jurisprudence, covering the major theories and arguments.

Slapper, Gary and Kelly, David. *English Law.* London: Cavendish, 2000. lxxxi, 967p. ISBN: 185941558X.

Covers all aspects of English law, including criminal law, contract, tort, consumer protection, equity and trusts. Examines the legal system in detail, including the funding of legal services. A website supports the book.

Slapper, Gary and Kelly, David. *The English Legal System* (5th edn, Cavendish Q and A Series). London: Cavendish, 2003. xviii, 270p. ISBN: 185941754X.

Explains what the law is and how the legal system operates and sets them in a social context. There is a passworded website for updates.

Slapper, Gary and Kelly, David. *Sourcebook on the English Legal System* (2nd edn). London: Cavendish, 2000. xxxiii, 583p. ISBN: 1859415539.

Updated to include the changes to the legal system, the book has a range of material, including statutes, cases, committee and commission reports, together with articles and commentaries.

Walker, David M. *The Scottish Legal System: An Introduction to the Study of Scots Law* (8th rev. edn). Edinburgh: W. Green, 2001. lv, 637p. ISBN: 0414013530.

Ward, Richard. *Walker and Walker's English Legal System* (8th edn). London: Butterworths, 1998. lx, 610p. ISBN: 0406996822.

Zander, Michael. *Cases and Materials on the English Legal System* (8th edn, Law in Context). London: Butterworths, 1999. xlvi, 689p. ISBN: 040692533X.

Zander, Michael. *The Law-Making Process* (5th edn, Law in Context). London: Butterworths, 1999. xliii, 458p. ISBN: 040690409X.

Journals

Journal of Law and Society. Oxford: Blackwell. ISSN: 0263-323X.

Continues *British Journal of Law and Society.*

Journal of Legal History. London: Frank Cass. ISSN: 0144-0365 (JLH).

The Publications of the Selden Society. London: Selden Society.

Excellent legal history source, with annual volumes having individual titles covering original source material never before in print, including early law reports, court records, judges' notebooks, legal treatises, precedents and practice books.

Volume 100 onwards is available from the Society. All the early volumes from 1 to 99 can be bought from American publisher W.S. Hein & Co. Inc.

There is an additional *Supplementary Series* which includes shorter works, bibliographies of manuscripts and lists identifying judges and lawyers.

Websites

Hotlinks: Legal History (*http://www.law.pitt.edu/hibbits/history*)

A very useful site by Bernard J. Hibbitts at the University of Pittsburgh School of Law, this has links to sites covering ancient law and American, English and European legal history.

Selden Society (*http://www.selden-society.qmw.ac.uk*)

The website of the society and publisher devoted to legal history. Has information about the society and membership. It includes a list of current publications and of the *Supplementary Series*.

8

Conflict of laws

English private law or conflict of laws is a body of rules which helps courts decide cases containing a foreign element. The important areas include jurisdiction and enforcement of foreign judgments, family questions such as marriage, matrimonial causes and children, and property disputes. Private law has seen considerable changes in case law and legislation and is increasingly dominated by legislation at the European and international level.

Books

Birks, Peter (ed.). *English Private Law* (Oxford English Law). Oxford: Oxford University Press, 2000. 2v. ISBN: 0198765002.

Written by a variety of expert contributors, this book looks at sources of law and principles of litigation and procedure and focuses on particular areas, the law of persons, property and obligations. Has been updated by a cumulative supplement.

Briggs, Adrian. *Civil Jurisdiction and Judgments* (3rd edn). London: LLP, 2002. lix, 665p. ISBN: 1859783740.

Briggs, Adrian. *The Conflict of Laws* (Clarendon Law Series). Oxford: Oxford University Press, 2002. xxxvii, 266p. ISBN: 0198763336.

Looks at whether the judgments of English courts are enforced and recognised overseas and also at the effect of foreign judgments in England. The principles of choice for cases with an international element are considered.

Clarkson, C.M.V. and Hill, Jonathan (2nd edn). *Jaffey on the Conflict of Laws*. London: Butterworths, 2002. xlv, 613p. ISBN: 0406942870.

For this edition, chapters on tort, jurisdiction and staying of actions have been updated and material on the Brussels and Lugano Conventions expanded.

Collier, J.G. *Conflict of Laws* (3rd edn). Cambridge: Cambridge University Press, 2001. lv, 403p. ISBN: 0521787815.

Dicey, Albert Venn and Morris, J.H.C. *Dicey and Morris on the Conflict of Laws* (13th edn). London: Sweet & Maxwell, 2000. 2v. ISBN: 0420482806.

Morris, J.H.C. *The Conflict of Laws* (5th edn by David Mclean). London: Sweet & Maxwell, 2000. lxxiv, 592p. ISBN: 0421661607.

Cover title: *Morris: The Conflict of Laws.*

North, Sir Peter and Fawcett, J.J. *Cheshire and North's Private International Law* (13th edn). London: Butterworths, 1999. cxxviii, 1,069p. ISBN: 0406905967.

O'Brien, John. *Conflict of Laws* (2nd edn). London: Cavendish, 1999. lxxx, 652p. ISBN: 1859412858.

Cover title: *Smith's Conflict of Laws.* First edition written by Raymond Smith. 1994.

Journals

International and Comparative Law Quarterly. Oxford: Oxford University Press [for] the British Institute of International and Comparative Law. ISSN: 0020-5893 (ICLQ).

Has some articles on private international law.

Websites

Hague Conference on International Law (*http://www.hcch.net/e/index.html*)

Site of the intergovernmental organisation working for the unification of private international law has publications, work in progress, conventions and member states.

Unidroit: Official Site of the International Institute for the Unification of Private Law (*http://www.unidroit.org/default.htm*)

Has details of the Institute's work, news and current work programme.

9

Constitutional and administrative law

This area, sometimes referred to as public law, is facing major change, including devolved powers to Scotland and Wales, new tiers of local government and regional agencies in England. The House of Lords is facing far-reaching reform and the Human Rights Act 1998, which is considered in more depth in the next chapter, is affecting public bodies by making them come into line with the European Convention on Human Rights. The courts may review administrative action and even parliamentary legislation in light of the Convention. On the horizon is the implementation of the Freedom of Information Act, the proposed abolition of the post of the Lord Chancellor and replacement of the Law Lords with a new American-style Supreme Court.

Books

Alder, John. *General Principles of Constitutional and Administrative Law* (4th edn, Palgrave Law Masters). Basingstoke: Palgrave Macmillan, 2002. xxxix, 598p. ISBN: 0333971647.

Previous edition published as: *Constitutional and Administrative Law.* 1999.

Allen, Michael J. and Thompson, Brian. *Cases and Materials on Constitutional and Administrative Law.* Oxford: Oxford University Press, 2002. xxxiii, 806p. ISBN: 0199255253.

Bagehot, Walter. *The English Constitution* (Oxford World's Classics). Oxford: Oxford University Press, 2001. xxxiv, 219p. ISBN: 0192839756.

Barnett, Hilaire A. *Constitutional and Administrative Law* (4th edn). London: Cavendish, 2002. xc, 1,026p. ISBN: 1859417213.

A favourite with students, this covers the main features of the constitution and looks at each layer of government, from local government to the European Union.

Blackburn, Robert, Kennon, Andrew with Wheeler-Booth, Michael. *Griffith and Ryle on Parliament: Functions, Practice and Procedures* (2nd edn). London: Sweet & Maxwell, 2003. xxiv, 805p. ISBN: 0421609109.

Brazier, Rodney. *Constitutional Practice: The Foundations of British Government* (3rd edn). Oxford: Oxford University Press, 1999. xx, 327p. ISBN: 0198298129.

Carroll, Alex. *Constitutional and Administrative Law* (2nd edn, The Foundation Studies in Law Series). Harlow: Pearson, 2002. xxxvii, 534p. ISBN: 058243808x.

Craig, P.P. *Administrative Law* (4th edn). London: Sweet & Maxwell, 1999. lxv, 922p. ISBN: 0421635908.

De Smith, Stanley and Brazier, Rodney. *Constitutional and Administrative Law* (8th edn). London: Penguin, 1998. xiii, 704p. ISBN: 0140258167.

De Smith, Stanley, Woolf, Lord and Jowell, Jeffrey. *De Smith, Woolf and Jowell's Principles of Judicial Review.* London: Sweet & Maxwell, 1999. cxxxvii, 720p. ISBN: 042162020X.

For students, an abridged and revised version of *Judicial Review of Administrative Action* (5th edn) by the same authors.

De Smith, Stanley, Woolf, Lord and Jowell, Jeffrey. *Judicial Review of Administrative Action* (5th edn). London: Sweet & Maxwell, 1998. 1,130p. ISBN: 042163880X.

Covers the history, principles and practice of judicial review. Has supplement.

Emery, Carl. *Administrative Law: Challenges to Official Action.* London: Sweet & Maxwell, 1999 (Sweet & Maxwell's Textbook Series). xxxix, 282p. ISBN: 0421620005.

Free online updates are available on Sweet & Maxwell's website.

Fenwick, Helen and Phillipson, Gavin. *Constitutional and Administrative Law* (4th edn, Cavendish Q and A Series). London: Cavendish, 2003. xxxiv, 399p. ISBN: 1859416225.

Revised to take into account constitutional reform since 1997, including devolution, reform of the House of the Lords and judicial review. Also covers the recent Shayler case under the Official Secrets Act.

Fenwick, Helen and Phillipson, Gavin. *Sourcebook on Public Law* (2nd edn). London: Cavendish, 2003. 1,150p. ISBN: 1859416551.

Fordham, Michael. *Judicial Review Handbook* (3rd edn). Oxford: Hart, 2001. 1,352p. ISBN: 1841132381.

Ganz, Gabriele. *Understanding Public Law* (3rd edn, Understanding Law). London: Sweet & Maxwell, 2001. 165p. ISBN: 0421635703.

Jowell, Jeffrey and Oliver, Dawn (eds). *The Changing Constitution* (4th edn). Oxford: Oxford University Press, 2000. xx, 387p. ISBN: 0198765738.

Review of recent developments by twelve expert contributors. Topics include devolution, the effect of the European Union, the reform of Parliament, changes to electoral systems and party funding.

Le Sueur, Andrew, Haerberg, Javan and English, Rosalind. *Principles of Public Law* (Cavendish Principles of Law Series). London: Cavendish, 1999. xlix, 584p. ISBN: 1859413811.

Lewis, N. Douglas. *Law and Governance: The Old Meets the New.* London: Cavendish, 2001. ix, 325p. ISBN: 1859415474.

How the traditional public law needs to adapt in the light of changes to the way the United Kingdom is governed, devolution and the move to broad-based administration.

Leyland, Peter and Woods, Terry. *Textbook on Administrative Law* (4th edn). Oxford: Oxford University Press, 2002. xxxv, 581p. ISBN: 0199255369.

Written with the general themes of accountability and citizen grievance claims running through the book. Covers European Union law and the section on judicial review has been rewritten, with a glossary of terms.

Loveland, Ian. *Constitutional Law: A Critical Introduction* (2nd edn). London: Butterworths, 2000. xxxv, 681p. ISBN: 0406915962.

Lyon, Ann. *Constitutional History of the UK.* London: Cavendish, 2003. xliii, 476p. ISBN: 1859417469.

Cover title: *Constitutional History of the United Kingdom.*

A very useful book for tracing the historical development of the British constitution, focusing on the political events and philosophical and religious ideas that have shaped the constitution. Has a companion website.

McEldowney, John F. *Public Law* (3rd edn, Sweet & Maxwell's Textbook Series). London: Sweet & Maxwell, 2002. xxxvi, 718p. ISBN: 0421780703.

Updated for the Human Rights Act 1998.

Mullen, Thomas J. *The Human Rights Act 1998 and Scots Law.* Glasgow: Legal Services Agency, 2001. xi, 132p.

Oliver, Dawn. *Constitutional Reform in the UK.* Oxford: Oxford University Press, 2003. xxi, 424p. ISBN: 0198765460.

Latest developments in constitutional law since the elections of 1997 and 2001 and the implications of these reforms for theories of democracy, citizenship, good governance and the increasingly important role of judges.

Phillips, O. Hood, Jackson, Paul and Leopold, Patricia. *O. Hood Phillips and Jackson: Constitutional and Administrative Law* (8th edn). London: Sweet & Maxwell, 2001. cxxvi, 855p. ISBN: 0421574801.

Previous edition published as: *O. Hood Phillips' Constitutional and Administrative Law*. 1987

Pollard, David, Parpworth, Neil and Hughes, David. *Constitutional and Administrative Law: Text with Materials* (3rd edn). London: Butterworths, 2001. xlviii, 983p. ISBN: 0406930562.

Supperstone, Michael and Knapman, Lynn (gen. eds). *Administrative Court Practice: Judicial Review.* London: Butterworths, 2002. xl, 236p. ISBN: 0406943532.

This has been endorsed by the Administrative Court as the official guide to judicial review. Covers all aspects of procedure, including appeals, interim relief and references to the European Court. Has appendices of court forms, notices and guidance notes.

Turpin, Colin C. *British Government and the Constitution: Text, Cases and Materials* (4th edn). London: Butterworths, 1999. xliv, 630p. ISBN: 0406988048.

Wade, Sir William and Forsyth, Christopher. *Administrative Law* (8th edn). Oxford: Oxford University Press, 2000. xc, 1,027p. ISBN: 0198765258.

Wallington, Peter and Lee, Robert G. (eds). *Blackstone's Statutes on Public Law and Human Rights.* Oxford: Oxford University Press, 2002. x, 581p. ISBN: 0199255350.

Useful statute book issued annually.

Law reports

Administrative Court Digest. London: Sweet & Maxwell. ISSN: 1473-4834 (ACD).

Formerly *Crown Office Digest*.

Administrative Law Reports. London: Butterworths. ISSN: 0957-9710 (Admin LR).

Journals

International Journal of Constitutional Law. Oxford: Oxford University Press with Hauser Global Law School Program, New York University. ISSN: 1474-2640 (I.CON).

A new academic quarterly journal covering comparative and international constitutional law.

Public Law. London: Sweet & Maxwell. ISSN: 0033-3565 (PL).

Includes digests and commentary on cases and legislation.

Websites

Constitution Unit (*http://www.ucl.ac.uk/constitution-unit*)

The website of the Constitution Unit, the British-based independent research body on constitutional reform, has a new look. Includes lists of publications and events and a useful site search engine. There are also links to relevant British government sites.

National Assembly for Wales (*http://www.wales.gov.uk/index.htm*)

Northern Ireland Assembly (*http://www.ni-assembly.gov.uk*)

The site for the currently suspended Assembly.

Scottish Parliament (*http://www.scottish.parliament.uk*)

Has general information and news and substantial resources, including annual reports, Bills, the work of committees, official reports, business bulletin and a weekly update.

United Kingdom Parliament (*http://www.parliament.uk*)

(See p. 37.)

10

Human rights

Since the Human Rights Act 1998, human rights no longer form a separate entity but are pervasive throughout the law. Human rights issues developed in one area of the law may be relevant to another, e.g. trial issues developed in family law may apply to criminal law cases. That said, much common law and statutory provision is in line with the standards in the European Convention and will not give rise to human rights questions.

Key topics in human rights are policing, public order and freedom of expression.

Books

United Kingdom law

Bailey, S.H., Harris, D.J. and Ormerod, D.C. *Civil Liberties: Cases and Materials* (5th edn). London: Butterworths, 2001. lxiii, 1,206p. ISBN: 0406903263.

Boyle, Alan. *Human Rights and Scots Law*. Oxford: Hart, 2002. xlix, 355p. ISBN: 1841130443.

Clayton, Richard and Tomlinson, Hugh. *The Law of Human Rights*. Oxford: Oxford University Press, 2002. 2v. ISBN: 019826223X.

Updated by supplements.

Feldman, David. *Civil Liberties and Human Rights in England and Wales* (2nd edn). Oxford: Oxford University Press, 2002. lxxvi, 1,108p. ISBN: 0198765037.

Considers the jurisprudence of the European Convention and discusses recent British legislation, including the Regulation of Investigatory Powers Act 2000. Also looks at new cases, including those involving prisoners and immigrants. A companion website supports the book.

Fenwick, Helen. *Civil Liberties and Human Rights* (3rd edn). London: Cavendish, 2002. ci, 1,149p. ISBN: 1859414931.

Critical analysis of the legal position of human rights and civil liberties in the United Kingdom, contrasted with other jurisdictions.

Grosz, Stephen, Beatson, Jack and Duffy, Peter. *Human Rights: The 1998 Act and the European Convention.* London: Sweet & Maxwell, 2000. lxv, 440p. ISBN: 0421630604.

Leckie, David and Pickersgill, David. *The 1998 Human Rights Act Explained.* London: Stationery Office, 1999. v, 95p. ISBN: 0117026840.

Useful for a quick guide, if slightly out of date.

Plowden, Philip and Kerrigan, Kevin. *Advocacy and Human Rights: Using the Convention in Courts and Tribunals.* London: Cavendish, 2002. liv, 440p. ISBN: 185941690X.

How to prepare and present European Convention based arguments before courts and tribunals.

Reed, Lord Robert John and Murdoch, Jim. *A Practical Guide to Human Rights in Scotland.* London: Sweet & Maxwell, 2001. lxx, 602p. ISBN: 0406923205.

Shorts, Edwin and De Than, Claire. *Human Rights Law in the UK.* London: Sweet & Maxwell, 2001. lxvii, 797p. ISBN: 0421754605.

This is a retitled new edition of *Civil Liberties: Legal Principles of Individual Freedom.* 1998.

Looks at the development of human rights in international law and at rights in Britain in the light of statutes such as the Terrorism Act 2000 and the Immigration and Asylum Act 1999 as well as the Human Rights Act. Has free online supplements at Sweet & Maxwell's website.

Spencer, Maureen and Spencer, John. *Human Rights.* London: Sweet & Maxwell, 2002. xv, 200p. ISBN: 0421767308.

Wadham, John and Mountfield, Helen. *Blackstone's Guide to the Human Rights Act 1998* (3rd edn). Oxford: Clarendon, 2002. 450p. ISBN: 0199254532.

Covers the main important British cases since incorporation of the European Convention into British law.

Whitty, Noel, Murphy, Therese and Livingstone, Stephen. *Civil Liberties Law: The Human Rights Act Era.* London: Butterworths, 2001. 499p. ISBN: 0406555117.

International law

Brownlie, Ian and Goodwin-Gill, Guy S. (eds). *Basic Documents on Human Rights* (4th edn). Oxford: Oxford University Press, 2002. xix, 896p. ISBN: 019924944X.

Collection of documents relating to human rights from the United Nations, its agencies, and regional and other organisations. Includes new treaties in emerging areas such as bio-ethics, and new protocols relating to women and children.

Mensah, Barbara. *European Human Rights Case Locator 1960–2000.*
London: Cavendish, 2000. xxi, 302p. ISBN: 185916489.

Basically, this lists the judgments of the European Court of Human Rights, arranging them in different ways for easy location and identification. There are lists putting the cases in alphabetical and chronological order and by article name and by country. This work stands alone or can be used with the author's *European Human Rights Case Summaries.*

Mensah, Barbara. *European Human Rights Case Summaries 1960–2000.*
London: Cavendish, 2001. xiv, 1,203p. ISBN: 1859416497.

Summaries of all the cases from the European Court of Human Rights, many of which have never been in United Kingdom law reports. To help find a case, there are subject lists and lists in chronological order. Copies of the relevant articles and protocols of the Convention are included.

Mowbray, A.R. *Cases and Materials on the European Convention of Human Rights.* London: Butterworths, 2001. 846p. ISBN: 040690328X.

After a chapter on the machinery of implementation, the book concentrates on the rights protected under the Convention.

O'Flaherty, Michael. *Human Rights and the UN: Practice Before the Treaty Bodies* (Nijhoff Law Specials, Vol. 54). The Hague and London: Nijhoff, 2002. xi, 226p. ISBN: 9041117881.

Recent book on the international position.

Ovey, Clare and White, Robin C.A. *Jacobs and White: The European Convention on Human Rights* (3rd edn). Oxford: Oxford University Press, 2002. xlvii, 506p. ISBN: 0198765800.

Covers both the procedure for making claims before the Strasbourg Court and the substantive law of the Convention. Includes recent cases, such as those covering the rights of transsexuals and airport noise at Heathrow.

Previously published as: *The European Convention on Human Rights.* 1996.

Rehman, Javaid. *International Human Rights Law: A Practical Approach.* Harlow: Longman, 2003. xlii, 494p. ISBN: 0582437733.

Smith, Rhona K.M. *Textbook on International Human Rights.* Oxford: Oxford University Press, 2003. xxxi, 361p. ISBN: 184743011.

Aimed at newcomers to the subject, there is an account of the development and history of human rights, including the role of the United Nations. Has examples from regional as well as international law and covers such contemporary issues as the right to education and freedom of expression.

Starmer, Keir. *Blackstone's Human Rights Digest.* London: Blackstone Press, 2001. lxi, 410p. ISBN: 1841741531.

Arranged by subject, the digest has extracts of cases from the key judgments of the European Commission and Court of Human Rights and cases from Commonwealth countries, including South Africa and New Zealand.

Has accompanying CD-Rom, which has the full text of all decisions of the European Court of Human Rights up to December 2000, and a supplement focusing on United Kingdom case law.

Steiner, Henry J. and Alston, Philip. *International Human Rights in Context: Law, Politics, Morals: Text and Materials* (2nd edn). Oxford: Oxford University Press, 2000. xxxiii, 1,497p. ISBN: 0198298498.

Strawson, John (ed.). *Law after Ground Zero.* London: Glasshouse, 2002. xxi, 222p. ISBN: 1904385028.

Looks at the emerging legal order since September 11th and considers the consequences for international human rights.

Law reports

European Human Rights Reports. London: Sweet & Maxwell. ISSN: 0260-4868 (EHRR).

Available on *Westlaw.*

Human Rights Reports: UK Cases. London: Sweet & Maxwell. ISSN: 1470-1669.

UK Human Rights Reports. Bristol: Jordans. ISSN: 1469-168X (UKHRR).

Also available as *United Kingdom Human Rights Reports Online (UKHRR Online)* (see p. 89).

Journals

European Human Rights Law Review. London: Sweet & Maxwell. ISSN: 1361-1526 (EHRLR).

Covers developments in British law.

Human Rights Alerter. London: Sweet & Maxwell. ISSN: 1470-3254.

Practitioner newsletter on the implementation of the Human Rights Act, with a digest of European and British human rights case law. Arranged by topic and issued ten times a year.

Online services

Human Rights (The Justis Databases)

Human Rights Direct

Part of *Butterworths LexisNexis Direct Services*, this includes British and European case law and legislation. It has Butterworths textbooks and an e-mail alerter.

Lawtel Human Rights Section

A section of *Lawtel*, this is an information service on the Human Rights Act.

United Kingdom Human Rights Reports Online (UKHRR Online)

From *Law Reports Online*, this has all of *UKHRR* from the first volume in 2000.

Websites

Charter 88: Unlocking Democracy (http://www.charter88.org.uk)

The website of the campaigning group Charter 88 has its papers on human rights and an A–Z of world constitutions, with links to almost every national and international convention in the world.

Commissioner for Human Rights (http://www.coe.int/T/E/Commissioner_H.R/ Communication_Unit/)

The site of the Council of Europe Office that promotes the awareness of human rights within the member states.

Council of Europe (http://www.coe.int/portalT.asp)

Includes a section on human rights.

European Court of Human Rights (http://www.echr.coe.int)

The Court's official site has a lot of useful information, including general material, basic texts relating to the Court, press releases, details of pending cases and judgments and decisions.

Human Rights Act 1998 (http://www.hmso.gov.uk/acts/acts1998/19980042.htm)

Unamended version of the Human Rights Act 1998.

Human Rights Update (http://www.humanrights.org.uk/5/text.nc)

This human rights site is run by barristers 1 Crown Office Row and has over 400 reports and commentaries on British human rights cases back to 1998. Updated weekly, the site also has articles as well as a forum and e-mail alerter service. Free registration.

Liberty (*http://www.liberty-human-rights.org.uk*)

The main site of Liberty, the London-based civil rights organisation.

Your Rights: The Liberty Guide to Human Rights (*http://www.yourrights.org.uk*)

This is a new site run by Liberty and it describes each article of the European Convention and considers how they are applied under the Human Rights Act. There is a news section.

11

Immigration law

The numbers of asylum and immigration appeals have been increasing over the last few years and there has been recent legislation with the Nationality, Immigration and Asylum Act 2002. Moreover, anyone giving advice on immigration must now be registered since the Immigration and Asylum Act 1999 which also set up a new system of welfare support.

Books

Blake, Nicholas and Husain, Raza. *Immigration, Asylum and the Human Rights Act 1998* (Blackstone's Human Rights Series). Oxford: Oxford University Press, 2003. lviii, 421p. ISBN: 184174140X.

Examines the working of the Human Rights Act in relation to British immigration law and looks at recent significant European cases.

Brennan, Rosie. *Immigration Advice at the Police Station* (2nd edn). London: Law Society, 2002. xvii, 300p. ISBN: 1853287474.

Previous edition: *Immigration Advice in the Police Station* by Michael Grewcock and Carolyn Taylor. 1995.
   This book is designed for lawyers who are not experts in immigration law but who have to deal with clients with immigration problems.

Cooray, Upali. *Cases and Materials on Immigration Law.* Aldershot: Ashgate, 2000. 325p. ISBN: 1855217708.

Jackson, David and Warr, George (gen. eds). *Immigration Law and Practice.* London: Sweet & Maxwell. Loose-leaf. ISBN: 0421747501.

MacDonald, Ian A. and Webber, Frances (gen. eds). *Immigration Law and Practice in the United Kingdom* (5th edn). London: Butterworths, 2001. cxlix, 1,724p. ISBN: 0406912742.

Cover title: *MacDonald's Immigration Law and Practice.*

Willman, Sue, Knafler, Stephen and Pierce, Stephen. *Support for Asylum-Seekers: A Guide to Legal and Welfare Rights.* London: Legal Action Group, 2001. xlvi, 543p. ISBN: 1903307023.

Covers asylum and immigration law and rights to housing, community care and welfare benefits. Includes extracts from the relevant legislation.

Law reports

Immigration and Nationality Law Reports. Bristol: Jordans. ISSN: 1460-423X (INLR).

Also available as *Immigration and Nationality Law Reports Online (INLR Online)* (see p. 93).

Immigration Appeals: Selected Reports of Decisions of the House of Lords, the Court of Appeal, the Court of Sessions and the High Court and Selected Determinations of the Immigration Appeal Tribunal under the Immigration Act 1971 and Related Legislation. London: Stationery Office. ISSN: 0966-758X (Imm AR).

Journals

Immigration, Asylum and Nationality Law (A Tolley Professional Journal). London: Reed Elsevier. ISSN: 0269-5774.

Continues: *Immigration and Nationality Law and Practice.*

International Journal of Refugee Law. Oxford: Oxford University Press. ISSN: 0953-8186 (IJRL).

As well as articles, has sections on cases and comments, developments and documents.
Available on *LexisNexis Professional*.

Online services

Immigration and Nationality Law Reports Online (INLR Online)

Part of Jordans' *Law Reports Online*, this has full text of the reports since they started in 1997.

Websites

Asylum Support Information: Your Resource for Asylum Support Information (http://www.asylumsupport.info/)

This site has useful information, including links to immigration law, although it is clearly a campaigning group.

EIN (Electronic Immigration Network) (http://www.ein.org.uk)

EIN is a voluntary sector organisation specialising in providing information on British and European immigration and refugee law. Some case law and legislation is available in the public part of the site but you would get most out of it by paying the annual fee to be a member.

Immigration and Nationality Directorate (http://www.ind.homeoffice.gov.uk)

The site of the Home Office directorate, responsible for immigration control at air and sea ports, has information for individuals applying for permission to stay, for citizenship or asylum.

Immigration, Work Visa and Work Permit Services (*http://www.workpermit .com*)

Previously BCL Immigration Services, this site includes a guide to UK permits, visas and immigration.

The Office of the Immigration Services Commissioner (OISC) Website (*http://www.oisc.org.uk/home.stm*)

The site of the independent body set up under the Immigration and Asylum Act 1999 to ensure that immigration advisers meet requirements of good practice. The site explains what the body does, including information on the requirements of work permit organisations to register.

UK Immigration Sources on the Internet (*http://www.analyticalq.com/ immigration/default.htm*)

Run by Anne Ku, this is a collection of useful links, if not kept as up to date as some sites.

12

Public revenue and taxation law

Substantial changes to the law were made by the Finance Act 2002, particularly in the area of corporation tax.

The various Tolleys and Simons publications dominate this field.

Books

United Kingdom law

Bramwell, Richard et al. *Taxation of Companies and Company Reconstructions* (8th edn). London: Sweet & Maxwell. Loose-leaf. ISBN: 0421827203.

Collison, David. *Simon's Tiley and Collison UK Tax Guide* (2002–2003, 20th edn). London: Tolley, 2002. xxvii, 2,111p. ISBN: 0406950296.

Dymond, Robert. *Dymond's Capital Taxes* (3rd edn). London: Gee. Loose-leaf. ISBN: 0851208517.

Schwarz, Jonathan. *Tax Treaties: United Kingdom Law and Practice.* London: Sweet & Maxwell, 2002. lviii, 287p. ISBN: 0421724900.

Simon's Capital Gains Tax Service. London: Butterworths. Loose-leaf. ISBN: 0406959641.

Simon's Corporation Tax Service. London: Butterworths. Loose-leaf. ISBN: 0406959676.

Simon's Direct Tax Service. London: Butterworths. ISBN: 0406897506 (non-folio loose-leaf and CD-Rom set).

Major subscription service for British and international taxation, the complete service including 12 loose-leaf volumes, *Butterworths Taxation Service* CD-Rom, *Budget Bulletin, Finance Bill Handbook, Finance Act Handbook, Simon's Tax Briefing Newsletter* and four Tolley annuals. There is the choice of alternative folio subscriptions, both hard copy and CD-Rom or just CD-Rom.

Tolley's Tax Series (including *Tolley's International Series*). Croydon: Tolley. Useful titles in this annual series include:

Tolley's Capital Gains Tax
Tolley's Corporation Tax
Tolley's Guide to Self-Assessment
Tolley's Income Tax
Tolley's Offshore Tax Planning
Tolley's Tax Planning
Tolley's Taxwise

Tookey, Michael (ed.). *Revenue Law* (3rd edn). London: Old Bailey Press, 2002. xxvii, 390p. ISBN: 1858364175.

Whitehouse, Chris and Narain, Lakshmi. *Revenue Law: Principles and Practice* (19th edn). London: Tolley, 2001. xlvii, 1,044p. ISBN: 0406939659.

Whiteman, Peter G. *Whiteman on Income Tax* (3rd edn, British Tax Library). London: Sweet & Maxwell, 1988. cxiii, 1,434p. ISBN: 0421347104.

Kept up to date by regular supplements. Previous edition published as: *Whiteman and Wheatcroft on Income Tax.* 1976.

Whiteman, Peter G., Gammie, Malcolm and Herbert, Mark. *Whiteman on Capital Gains Tax* (4th edn, British Tax Library). London: Sweet & Maxwell, 1988. l, 834p. ISBN: 0421372605.

Updated by supplements. Previous edition published as: *Whiteman and Wheatcroft on Capital Gains Tax.* 1980.

European law

Terra, Ben and Wattel, Peter. *European Tax Law* (3rd edn). London: Kluwer Law International, 2001. xx, 532p. ISBN: 9041198687.

Law reports

British Tax Cases. London: Croner.CCH Group. ISBN: 0863250033 (loose-leaf and annual vol.) (BTC).

Annual volumes supported by loose-leaf volumes.

There is an alternative CD-Rom version as part of CCH's *Electronic Library*, which has the full text of cases since 1999, case tables and *Taxes: The Weekly Tax News*.

Reports of Tax Cases. London: Butterworths. ISBN: 040699871X (set).

Cover title: *Tax Cases*. Has indexes.

Simon's Tax Cases. London: Butterworths. ISSN: 0308-8030 (STC).

Supported by current service, including cumulative lists and indexes. Fully cross-referenced to *Simon's Direct Tax Service* and other Butterworths encyclopaedic works. Also available as *Butterworths Taxation Service* CD-Rom.

Value Added Tax and Duties Tribunals Reports. London: Stationery Office.

Journals

British Tax Review. London: Sweet & Maxwell. ISSN: 0007-1870 (BTR).

Simon's Tax Briefing. London: Butterworths. ISSN: 1468-9014.

Simon's Weekly Tax Intelligence. London: Butterworths. ISSN: 1357-7905.

Complements *Simon's Direct Tax Service* by providing a weekly service for developments in direct and indirect taxation. Has cumulative lists and indexes and a special budget issue. It is also available on CD-Rom.

Simon's Weekly Tax Service. London: Butterworths.

Weekly updates covering the previous week's developments in the taxation field. Includes detailed summaries of cases and full texts of statutory instruments and press releases.

Online services

Tax Services

Part of *Butterworths LexisNexis Direct Services.*

Websites

HM Customs and Excise (http://www.hmce.gov.uk)

Has information about value added tax for businesses and for the public, particularly travellers. Also has a section on what the Commissioners do and links to more about VAT.

Inland Revenue (http://www.inlandrevenue.gov.uk)

News and information on tax and national insurance. Has separate sections for businesses, employers, charities and practitioners. The latter section includes the tax bulletin, internal manuals, budget information and statutes.

13

Employment and industrial relations law

The Employment Act was passed in 2002 and there are proposed changes to disciplinary and grievance procedures as well as plans by the British government for more flexible working hours for working parents. Moreover, new maternity regulations will give greater rights to expectant mothers. Generally, there is an increasing involvement by European law, such as the directive on fixed-term work.

Books

United Kingdom law

Anderman, S.D. *The Law of Unfair Dismissal* (3rd edn). London: Butterworths, 2001. lix, 492p. ISBN: 0406921814.

Arora, Vinita and Nicholls, Paul. *Employment Tribunals: Presenting a Winning Case.* London: Gee Publishing, 2000. 28p.

Short guide to employment tribunals.

Barnett, Daniel and Scrope, Henry. *Employment Law Handbook.* London: Law Society, 2002. xlii, 374p. ISBN: 1853287164.

Covers recent changes including the Employment Bill 2002, has the fully amended and complete text of the Employment Rights Act 1996 and examines managing disciplinary and grievance procedures.

Barrow, Charles et al. *Blackstone's Guide to the Employment Relations Act 1999*. London: Blackstone Press, 2001. xxi, 256p. ISBN: 1841741256.

Explains the meaning of the provisions and has some background briefing regarding the legislative objectives.

Barrow, Charles. *Industrial Relations Law* (2nd edn). London: Cavendish, 2002. 392p. ISBN: 1859415636.

Updated to include the Employment Relations Act 1999 and the Human Rights Act. Covers the historical development of the law and the economic and industrial influences on it.

Belitz, Hina and Crossley-Holland, Dominic. *The Penguin Guide to Employment Rights*. London: Penguin, 2002. x, 330p. ISBN: 0141000457.

Practical guide for employees.

Blanpain, Roger. *European Labour Law* (8th rev. edn). The Hague and London: Kluwer International, 2002. 664p. ISBN: 9041118489.

Bowers, John. *Bowers on Employment Law* (6th edn). Oxford: Oxford University Press, 2002. lxxviii, 624p. ISBN: 0199254516.

New edition of *Employment Law*. 2000. Covers individual and collective labour law and has analysis of the Human Rights Act.

Casserley, Catherine and Gor, Bela. *Disability Discrimination Claims: An Adviser's Handbook*. Bristol: Jordans, 2001. xxvii, 261p. ISBN: 0853086427.

Collins, Hugh, Ewing, K.D. and McColgan, Aileen. *Labour Law: Text and Materials*. Oxford: Hart, 2001. xlviii, 1,093p. ISBN: 1841132365.

Cracknell, D.G. *Employment Law* (2nd edn, Cracknell's Statutes). London: Old Bailey Press, 2003. xvii, 645p. ISBN: 1858364752.

Cushway, Barry. *The Employer's Handbook: An Essential Guide to Employment Law, Personnel Policies and Procedures.* London: Kogan Page, 2002. x, 320p. ISBN: 0749436980.

Accompanied by CD-Rom.

Deakin, Simon and Morris, Gillian S. *Labour Law* (3rd edn). London: Butterworths, 2001. lxxv, 1,081p. ISBN: 0406915989.

Hammond Suddards (firm). *Employment Relations Act* (Legal Essentials). London: Institute of Personnel and Development, 2000. lx, 42p. ISBN: 0852928505.

Harvey, R.J. *Harvey on Industrial Relations and Employment Law.* London: Butterworths. Loose-leaf. ISBN: 0406221731.

Loose-leaf and has updating bulletin with it.

Jefferson, Michael. *Principles of Employment Law* (4th edn). London: Cavendish, 2000. lxxv, 570p. ISBN: 1859414680.

Emphasis on substantive and procedural topics, such as express and implied terms, unfair dismissal and discrimination. Examines the defects in the law.

New edition to be published (see publisher's website: *http://www.cavendish publishing.com*).

Kibling, Thomas and Lewis, Tamara. *Employment Law: An Advisers' Handbook* (4th edn). London: Legal Action Group. lii, 456p. ISBN: 0905099931.

Kidner, Richard. *Blackstone's Statutes on Employment Law.* Oxford: Oxford University Press.

Annual.

Lewis, David and Sargeant, Malcolm. *Essentials of Employment Law* (7th edn, People and Organisations). London: Chartered Institute of Personnel and Development, 2002. xxx, 369p. ISBN: 0852929390.

Updated and comprehensive, including parental rights, working time, data protection and trade union issues.

Lockton, Deborah. *Employment Law* (3rd edn, Cavendish Q and A Series). London: Cavendish, 2002. xxx, 271p. ISBN: 1859417477.

Covers recent decisions by United Kingdom courts and the European Court of Justice and has the changes brought about by European directives, such as time work discrimination and fixed-time work, and the Employment Act 2002, which have affected institutions, employment protection, equal opportunity and unfair dismissal.

Mackay, Malcolm R. and Simon, Shona M.W. *Employment Law* (2nd edn). Edinburgh: W. Green, 2001. xlvii, 376p. ISBN: 0414014022.

Scottish employment law.

McMullen, Jeremy, Eady, Jennifer and Tuck, Rebecca. *Employment Tribunal Procedure: A Users' Guide to Tribunals and Appeals* (2nd edn). London: Legal Action Group, 2002. l, 548p. ISBN: 1903307074.

O'Dempsey, Declan et al. *Employment Law and the Human Rights Act 1998.* Bristol: Jordans, 2001. lii, 374p. ISBN: 085308503X.

Examines the compatibility of British employment law with the European Convention on Human Rights, including trade union law and unfair dismissal.

Osman, Christopher (gen. ed.). *Butterworths Employment Law Guide* (3rd edn). London: Butterworths, 2000. lxxii, 853p. ISBN: 0406904936.

Painter, Richard W. and Holmes, Ann. *Cases and Materials on Employment Law* (4th edn). Oxford: Oxford University Press, 2002. liii, 952p. ISBN: 0199254818.

Updated to cover new developments in relation to transfer of undertakings, equal pay, discrimination and health and safety.

Palmer, Camilla. *Discrimination Law Handbook.* London: Legal Action Group, 2002. 1,264p. ISBN: 1903307139.

Covers British, European and human rights law relating to discrimination.

Pitt, Gwyneth. *Employment Law* (4th edn). London: Sweet & Maxwell, 2000. lxvi, 497p. ISBN: 0421690100.

Fifth edition to be published (see publisher's website: *http://www.smlawpub .co.uk*).

Rubenstein, Michael. *Discrimination: A Guide to the Relevant Case Law on Sex, Race and Disability Discrimination and Equal Pay* (16th edn). London: Butterworths, 2003. 114p. ISBN: 0406964289.

Rubenstein, Michael and Frost, Yvonne. *Unfair Dismissal: A Guide to Relevant Case Law* (20th edn). London: Eclipse Group for Industrial Relations Services, 2002. 120p. ISBN: 0406956936.

Twenty-first edition to be published by Butterworths (*http://www.butterworths .co.uk*).

Selwyn, Norman. *Law of Employment* (11th edn). London: Butterworths, 2000. lxxxiv, 706p. ISBN: 0406913579.

Slade Elizabeth A. [with] members of 11 King's Bench Walk Chambers. *Tolley's Employment Handbook*. Croydon: Tolley, 2001. lxxxv, 794p. ISBN: 0754512665.

Smith, I.T. and Thomas, Gareth. *Industrial Law* (8th edn). London: Butterworths, 2000. lxxviii, 779p. ISBN: 0406904111.

Cover title: *Smith and Wood's Industrial Law*. Includes health and safety at work and social security law as it affects employment.

Ninth edition to be published (see publisher's website *http://www .butterworths.co.uk*).

Tolley's Employment Service. London: Tolley.

CD-Rom subscription, with password.

Waite, John-Paul, Isted, Barry and Payne, Alan. *Tolley's Employment Tribunals Handbook: Practice, Procedure and Strategies for Success*. London: Tolley, 2002. xix, 348p. ISBN: 0754514889.

Wallington, Peter. *Butterworths Employment Law Handbook* (10th edn). London: Butterworths, 2002. xv, 2,102p. ISBN: 040694878X.

European law

Barnard, Catherine. *EC Employment Law* (2nd edn, Oxford EC Law Library). Oxford: Oxford University Press, 2000. cv, 600p. ISBN: 0198765657.

Kenner, Jeff. *EU Employment Law: From Rome to Amsterdam and Beyond.* Oxford: Hart, 2003. liii, 593p. ISBN: 1901362698.

Law reports

Industrial Cases Reports. London: Incorporated Council of Law Reporting for England and Wales. ISSN: 0306-2163 (ICR).

The reports cover employment law, discrimination and competition.

Complementary to the reports is a new free web-based service *The Industrial Cases Reports Express* at *http://www.lawreports.co.uk/ICREhome.htm.* This updating service, similar to *The Daily Law Notes,* has brief summaries of the cases as soon as the headnotes are available and sometimes before the full cases are in the reports.

Appears on *The Justis Databases.*

Industrial Relations Law Reports. London: Butterworths. ISSN: 0307-5591 (IRLR).

Also available on CD-Rom as *eIRLR*, on *Butterworth's Employment Law Online* (see p. 105) and on *Westlaw.*

Journals

Industrial Law Journal. Oxford: Oxford University Press for the Industrial Law Society. ISSN: 0355-9332 (Ind LJ).

Available on *LexisNexis Professional.*

The International Journal of Comparative Labour Law and Industrial Relations. Deventer: Kluwer. ISSN: 0952-617X.

Online services

Employment Law Online

Part of *Butterworths LexisNexis Direct Services*, this has the *Industrial Relations Law Reports*, selected *All England Law Reports* and unreported cases. *Harvey on Industrial Relations and Employment Law* can also be included in the subscription.

EOR Direct.Com

Also part of *Butterworths LexisNexis Direct Services*, this covers equal opportunity law.

Websites

Acas (http://www.acas.org.uk)

The website for the Advisory, Conciliation and Arbitration Service has news, events, press releases and details of the service's helpline. Most usefully, it has an employment topics section, with summaries of the law and links to pdf files of more detailed information. Current topics aimed at the general public include flexible hours and new rights for working parents.

Emplaw (*http://www.emplaw.co.uk*)

Has a free area of basic information on British employment law and links to relevant books on Amazon and to employment law and official sites. More detailed information is available by subscription, with a daily and weekly pass among the options.

Employment Appeal Tribunal (*http://www.employmentappeals.gov.uk*)

Has information about the tribunal, practice directions, notes about appealing, cause list and judgments.

Jobsworth.com: Online Employment Contracts and Policies (*http://www .jobsworth.com*)

Has priced online employment contracts, free downloadable legal information on employment issues and a glossary of employment terms. It is possible to register for an e-mail service for the latest information.

Thompsons Solicitors (*http://www.thompsons.law.co.uk*)

Run by Thompsons Solicitors who act for trade union members with cases involving employment rights. Has useful information and the monthly *Thompsons Labour and European Review* is downloadable as a pdf file.

14

Environmental law

Environmental law is one of the quickest changing areas of the law. There are significant trends, including the Human Rights Act, the increasing public awareness of environmental issues and the greater importance of international law. Important legal developments include the Pollution Prevention and Control Act 1999, the enactment of the European Union Directive on IPPC, the Landfill Regulations 2002 and the Contaminated Land Regulations 2000.

Books

United Kingdom law

Bell, Stuart and McGillivray, Donald. *Ball and Bell on Environmental Law: The Law and Policy Relating to the Protection of the Environment* (5th edn). London: Blackstone Press, 2000. xlviii, 726p. ISBN: 185431887X.

Well-established work on the topic, which has been rewritten to cover contaminated land, environmental values and the Climate Change Treaty.

Duxbury, Robert M.C. and Morton, Sandra G. *Blackstone's Statutes on Environmental Law*. Oxford: Oxford University Press.

Annual.

Garbutt, John. *Environmental Law: A Practical Handbook* (3rd edn). Bembridge: Palladian Law, 2000. xxv, 175p. ISBN: 1902558243.

Gilpin, Alan. *Dictionary of Environmental Law*. Cheltenham: Edward Elgar, 2000. 377p. ISBN: 1840641886.

Harris, D.J. (ed.). *Garner's Environmental Law*. London: Butterworths. Loose-leaf. ISBN: 0406996156.

Annotated British and European Union sources on environmental law arranged by subject. Includes primary and secondary legislation, European Union directives, British government circulars and forms and precedents.

Hellawell, Trevor. *Environmental Law Handbook* (5th edn). London: Law Society, 2002. xx, 259p. ISBN: 1853288918.

Hughes, David et al. *Environmental Law* (4th edn). London: Butterworths, 2002. lxxii, 725p. ISBN: 0406942919.

Aimed at non-specialists, this book looks at how environmental law affects everyday property, financial and business transactions and includes environmental liabilities and searches, contaminated land insurance and the Environmental Liability Directive.

Ong, David M., Sunkin, Maurice and Wright, Robert. *Sourcebook on Environmental Law* (2nd edn). London: Cavendish, 2001. lxxvi, 901p. ISBN: 1859415865.

Selection of sources of international, European and British law. Has comments and references to other resources, including websites.

Reid, Colin T. *Nature Conservation Law* (2nd edn). Edinburgh: W. Green, 2002. lix, 429p. ISBN: 0414013557.

Scottish law.

Wolf, Susan, White, Anna and Stanley, Neil. *Principles of Environmental Law* (3rd edn, Cavendish Principles of Law Series). London: Cavendish, 2002. lxii, 513p. ISBN: 1859415814.

Covers British and European law and regulatory control and considers the overlap between planning and environmental regulation.

European law

Jans, Jan H. *European Environmental Law* (2nd rev. edn). Amsterdam: Europa Law Publishing, 2000. 464p. ISBN: 9076871019.

Kramer, Ludwig. *EC Environmental Law* (4th edn). London: Sweet & Maxwell, 2000. xxxvii, 329p. ISBN: 0421590203.

New edition of: *EC Treaty and Environmental Law*. 1998.

Law reports

Environmental Law Reports. London: Sweet & Maxwell. ISSN: 0966-2022 (Env LR).

Full reports and digests of cases from the United Kingdom and the Court of Justice of the European Communities. Available on *Westlaw*.

Journals

Journal of Environmental Law. Oxford: Oxford University Press. ISSN: 0952-8873.

Available on *LexisNexis Professional*.

Yearbook of European Environmental Law. Oxford: Oxford University Press.

A collaboration between academics, practitioners and officials from the European Union, this annual survey covers developments in environmental law at both European and national level.

Websites

Ecolex: A Gateway to Environmental Law (*http://www.ecolex.org*)

This may prove useful for international law, although it is a new site and still in development. Includes information, rather than full text, on multilateral treaties, court decisions and European Union law.

English Nature (*http://www.english-nature.org.uk*)

The government agency for the conservation of wildlife and geology in England has news, environmental policy, press releases and position statements.

Environment Agency (*http://www.environment-agency.gov.uk*)

This has useful information about the Agency and what it does. It also has news and the texts of recent publications, including guidance notes.

European Environmental Law Home Page (*http://www.eel.nl*)

Has cases, legislation and other material relating to European environmental law. Visitors can subscribe to a free news service to receive latest changes to the site by e-mail. A small charge is being considered for this in the future.

PaceVirtual Environmental Law Page (*http://law.pace.edu/env/vell6.html*)

This site, run by Robert J. Goldstein at Pace University School of Law, is strongest for international law, with information on the important treaties. It does also have a comparative law section, with links to sites on European and British law.

Scottish Environment Protection Agency (SEPA) (*http://www.sepa.org.uk*)

The site for the body responsible for the protection of the environment in Scotland has news and publications, policy guidance and information on their regulatory work.

15

Planning law

Planning law is still a very confusing area, despite attempts to simplify it. Changes are coming with the Planning and Compulsory Purchase Bill going through Parliament. The Human Rights Act 1998 has been considered in some cases, including deciding whether the way the Secretary of State recovered jurisdiction of planning appeals was in breach of the European Convention.

Books

Brand, Clive. *Planning Law* (4th edn, Practice Notes). London: Cavendish, 2001. 148p. ISBN: 1859414540.

Straightforward guide to making a planning application, including the appeal procedure.

Moore, Victor. *A Practical Approach to Planning Law* (8th edn). Oxford: Oxford University Press, 2002. xlv, 680p. ISBN: 0199255954.

Covers recent cases brought under the Human Rights Act and all aspects of planning law, including remedies for adverse planning decisions and conservation of natural habitats.

Moore, Victor and Hughes, David (eds). *Blackstone's Statutes on Planning Law* (3rd edn, Blackstone's Statute Books). London: Blackstone Press, 2000. 550p. ISBN: 1841740942.

Includes the principal legislative materials, including the Environment Act 1995 and the major changes to the Town and Country Planning Act 1990 introduced by the Greater London Authority Act 1999.

Rowan-Robinson, Jeremy et al. *Scottish Planning Law and Procedure* (2nd edn). Edinburgh: W. Green under the auspices of Scottish Universities Law Institute, 2001. xvix, 888p. ISBN: 0414014308.

Scottish planning law.

Telling, A.E. *Telling and Duxbury's Planning Law and Procedure* (12th edn). London: Butterworths, 2002. xx, 533p. ISBN: 0406947961.

Law reports

JPL Planning Law Case Reports. London: Sweet & Maxwell.

Previously issued as *Planning Law Case Reports*, the four issues a year cover cases which cannot be fitted into the case reports section of the *Journal of Planning and Environment Law*.

Journals

Journal of Planning and Environment Law. London: Sweet & Maxwell. ISSN: 0307-4870.

Previously published as the *Journal of Planning and Property Law*.

Websites

Planning Inspectorate (*http://www.planning-inspectorate.gov.uk*)

Has the rules for planning appeals, information on planning generally, rights of way and how purchase notices work. Also has the Agency's annual reports and links to the Countryside and Rights of Way Act 2000, which requires statutory bodies to prepare maps of open country.

Planning Portal (*http://www.planningportal.gov.uk/wps/portal*)

Live since May 2002, this British government site links public, business and other users to a wide range of advice, guidance and services on planning and related topics.

Internet and computer law

Internet and computer law is a rapidly changing area, as the technology and regulation of the Internet, telecommunications and broadcasting come closer together. Key areas include property rights and data protection. Intellectual property law (see p. 167) is relevant too. E-commerce books are listed in Chapter 28 on business law.

Books

Bainbridge, David I. *Introduction to Computer Law* (4th edn). Harlow: Longman, 2000. xxx, 480p. ISBN: 0582423341.

Examines the law in the context of the practicalities of computer use. Covers data protection, computer misuse and database rights.

Black, Sharon K. *Telecommunications Law in the Internet Age* (The Morgan Kaufmann Series in Networking). San Francisco and London: Morgan Kaufmann, 2002. xix, 516p. ISBN: 1558605460.

Kevan, Tim and McGrath, Paul. *E-mail, the Internet and the Law: Essential Knowledge for Safer Surfing.* Welwyn Garden City: EMIS Professional, 2001. xvi, 223p. ISBN: 1858112680.

The legal implications of e-mail.

Lederman, Eli and Shapira, Ron. *Law, Information and Information Technology* (Law and Electronic Commerce; Vol. 13). The Hague and London: Kluwer Law International, 2001. xvi, 429p. ISBN: 9041116753.

Lloyd, Ian J. *Information Technology Law* (3rd edn). London: Butterworths, 2000. xlvii, 634p. ISBN: 0406914893.

Covers data protection and computer crime and considers the effectiveness of intellectual property law in protecting electronic rights and products. The book has an associated web page.

Phillips, Jeremy (consultant ed.). *Butterworths E-commerce and IT Law Handbook*. London: Butterworths, 2000. xiv, 1,564p. ISBN: 0406934312.

New edition of *Butterworths Information Technology Law Handbook*. 1998.

Reed, Chris. *Internet Law: Text and Materials*. London: Butterworths, 2000. xxviii, 280p. ISBN: 0406981418.

Second edition to be published (see publisher's website *http://www .butterworths.co.uk*).

Reed, Chris and Angel, John (eds). *Computer Law* (4th edn). London: Blackstone Press, 2000. xliii, 515p. ISBN: 1841740160.

Introduction to the law relating to the use of computer technology.

  Fifth edition to be published by Oxford University Press (see publisher's website *http://www.oup.com*).

Smith, J.H. (ed.). *Internet Law and Regulation* (3rd edn). London: Sweet & Maxwell, 2002. xlvii, 737p. ISBN: 0421705906.

Walden, Ian and Angel, John (eds). *Telecommunications Law*. London: Blackstone Press, 2001. xxx, 547p. ISBN: 1841741213.

Looks at the law and regulations relating to telecommunications, nationally and internationally. Covers Britain, America, the European Union and the Far East.

Law reports

Information Technology Law Reports. Witney: Lawtext. ISSN: 1365-8867 (Info TLR).

Covers Australian and European cases on the topic as well as those from Britain.

Journals

International Journal of Law and Information Technology. Oxford: Oxford University Press. ISSN: 0967-0769 (IJLT).

Articles on computer law, covering such topics as computer misuse, intellectual property rights and computer contracts, and on the use of computers in the law office, for example for litigation support and cash-flow management.

Websites

JILT: Journal of Information Law and Technology (*http://elj.warwick.ac.uk/jilt/default.htm*)

Web journal by the Electronic Law Journals Project at Warwick Law School has wide-ranging articles on e-commerce, information technology and the Internet, intellectual property and legal education using the web.

Oftel: Office of Telecommunications (*http://www.oftel.gov.uk*)

The site for the regulator of the United Kingdom telecommunications industry has separate sections on consumer and industry information. The latter includes the implementation of European directives.

Society for Computers and Law (*http://www.scl.org/default.asp*)

The site for the Society for Computers and Law, the British organisation concerned with the encouragement and development of law-related IT and IT-related law, has news and articles on latest developments.

17

Criminal law

The British government is proposing a large shake-up of the criminal justice system, with changes to the double jeopardy rule and a crackdown on anti-social behaviour. The Criminal Justice Bill is before Parliament and there has been some significant recent legislation, with the Criminal Justice (Theft and Fraud Offences) Act 2001, the Proceeds of Crime Act 2002, the Anti-Terrorism, Crime and Security Act 2001, the Police Reform Act 2002 and the Mobile Telephones Reprogramming Act 2002. The Electronic Signatures Regulations 2002 are also important and the European Convention on Human Rights is having an impact on some criminal law cases.

Books

Allen, Christopher. *Evidence* (5th edn, Cavendish Q and A Series). London: Cavendish, 2002. xxvi, 224p. ISBN: 1859417361.

Looks at criminal evidence and considers the importance of the Human Rights Act in relation to reverse burdens of proof, improperly obtained evidence and s. 41 of the Youth Justice and Criminal Evidence Act 1999.

Allen, Michael J. *Textbook on Criminal Law* (7th edn). London: Oxford University Press, 2003. 560p. ISBN: 0199260699.

Archbold: Criminal Pleading, Evidence and Practice. London: Sweet & · Maxwell.

For practitioners in the Crown Court, it covers court procedure and offences. The main work is updated and supported by supplements, including the *Criminal Appeals Index*. Also available on CD-Rom.

Blackstone's Criminal Practice. Oxford: Oxford University Press.

Issued annually, this is designed to cover material needed for criminal practice in one volume, with the emphasis on the Magistrates' and Crown Courts. Has all criminal statutes and practice directions. Also available as a CD-Rom and as part of *Crime Online* (see p. 124).

Card, Richard. *Criminal Law* (15th edn). London: Butterworths, 2001. lx, 746p. ISBN: 0406934010.

Cheney, Deborah et al. *Criminal Justice and the Human Rights Act 1998* (2nd edn). Bristol: Jordans, 2001. xxxv, 276p. ISBN: 0853087245.

Clarkson, C.M.V. *Understanding Criminal Law* (3rd edn, Understanding Law). London: Sweet & Maxwell, 2001. 321p. ISBN: 0421717505.

Cousens, Michael and Blair, Ruth (eds). *Butterworths Police and Criminal Evidence Act Cases.* London: Butterworths. Loose-leaf. ISBN: 0406996490.

Eady, David and Smith, A.T.H. *Arlidge, Eady and Smith on Contempt* (2nd edn, The Common Law Library). London: Sweet & Maxwell, 1999. cxlvii, 1,191p. ISBN: 0421459107.

Cumulative supplements to this have been published.

Elliot, Catherine and Quinn, Frances. *Criminal Law* (4th edn). Harlow: Longman, 2002. xxii, 344p. ISBN: 0582473128.

Gane, Christopher and Stoddart, Charles N. *A Casebook on Scottish Criminal Law* (3rd edn). Edinburgh: W. Green, 2001. xlvii, 620p. ISBN: 0414010507.

Geary, Roger. *Understanding Criminal Law.* London: Cavendish, 2002. 134p. ISBN: 1859417493.

Evaluates the current law and suggests possible reforms.

Glazebrook, P.R. *Blackstone's Statutes on Criminal Law.* London: Blackstone Press.

Annual.

Gordon, Gerald H. with Christie, Michael G.A. (ed.). *The Criminal Law of Scotland Vol. 1* (3rd edn). Edinburgh: W. Green [for] Scottish Universities Law Institute, 2000. liv, 541p. ISBN: 0414010566.

Gordon, Gerald H. with Christie, Michael G.A. (ed.). *The Criminal Law of Scotland Vol. 2* (3rd edn). Edinburgh: W. Green [for] Scottish Universities Law Institute, 2001. xcvi, 801p. ISBN: 0414013999.

Herring, Jonathan. *Criminal Law* (3rd edn, Palgrave Law Masters). Basingstoke: Palgrave Macmillan, 2002. xxxii, 485p. ISBN: 0333987705.

Hungerford-Welch, Peter. *Criminal Litigation and Sentencing* (5th edn). London: Cavendish, 2000. lxxxiii, 905p. ISBN: 1859415598.

Jago, Robert. *A–Z Companion to Criminal Law.* London: Cavendish Press, 2003. 430p. ISBN: 1859417035.

Magistrates' Courts Criminal Practice. Bristol: Jordans.

Annual, covering practice and procedure in the magistrates' court, with annotated statutes. Has accompanying CD-Rom version of the book.

Matthews, Paul. *Jervis on the Office and Duties of Coroners: with Forms and Precedents* (12th edn). London: Sweet & Maxwell, 2002. xxxiii, 927p. ISBN: 042178010X.

May, Richard. *Criminal Evidence* (4th edn). London: Sweet & Maxwell, 1999. lxxvii, 568p. ISBN: 0421589507.

There are free online updates on Sweet & Maxwell's website. New edition is expected soon (see publisher's website *http://www.smlawpub.co.uk*).

Norrie, Alan W. *Crime, Reason and History: A Critical Introduction to Criminal Law* (2nd edn, Law in Context). London: Butterworths, 2001. xxv, 274p. ISBN: 0406932468.

Smith, John Cyril. *Smith and Hogan Criminal Law* (10th edn). London: Butterworths, 2002. c, 807p. ISBN: 0406948011.

Previous edition by John Cyril Smith and Brian Hogan, 1999. Covers general principles of criminal liability and the law of the most important crimes. Includes a new short account of money-laundering. Cross-referenced to *Smith and Hogan Criminal Law Cases and Materials*.

Smith, John Cyril and Hogan, Brian. *Smith and Hogan Criminal Law: Cases and Materials* (8th edn). London: Butterworths, 2002. liv, 781p. ISBN: 0406948003.

Accompanying casebook.

Sprack, John. *Emmins on Criminal Procedure* (9th edn). Oxford: Oxford University Press, 2002. xlviii, 562p. ISBN: 0199253501.

Practical guide, following the procedure right through from the start of criminal proceedings to the final appeal. Covers summary trial in the magistrates' court, trial on indictment, sentencing and appeals. Includes a model brief.

Starmer, Keir, Strange, Michael and Whitaker, Quincy. *Criminal Justice, Police Powers and Human Rights* (Blackstone's Human Rights Series). London: Blackstone Press, 2001. xli, 338p. ISBN: 1841741388.

Applies the European Convention and the Human Rights Act to criminal law.

Stone's Justices' Manual. London: Butterworths.

Annual guide to magistrates' courts and their procedure, covering statutes and practice directions. Also published as *Stone's Justices' Manual Direct* (see p. 124).

Storey, Tony and Lidbury, Alan. *Criminal Law*. Cullompton: Willan, 2001. xxiii, 407p. ISBN: 1903240255.

Uglow, Steve et al. *Criminal Justice* (2nd edn). London: Sweet & Maxwell, 2002. xxix, 474p. ISBN: 0421738405.

Wasik, Martin. *Emmins on Sentencing* (4th edn). Oxford: Oxford University Press, 2001. 456p. ISBN: 1841742457.

A guide to the sentences which are available to the courts, covering practice in the Crown Court and magistrates' court. This edition has been rewritten to take into account the Powers of Criminal Courts (Sentencing) Act 2000 and the introduction of exclusion, disqualification and drug abstinence orders under the Criminal Justice and Court Services Act 2000.

Law reports

Cox's Reports of Cases in Criminal Law Argued and Determined in the Courts of England. London: Butterworths (Cox CC).

Alternative title: *Cox's Criminal Law Cases.*
  A source for older cases, this covers 1843–1941.
  Available on *Westlaw.*

Criminal Appeal Reports. London: Sweet & Maxwell. ISSN: 0070-1521 (Cr App R).

Available on *Westlaw* and *The Justis Databases.*

Road Traffic Reports. London: Sweet & Maxwell. ISSN: 0038-1047 (RTR).

Journals

Criminal Law Review. London: Sweet & Maxwell. ISSN: 0011-135X (Crim LR).

As well as articles, the journal has case reports. In searching for these, students tend to mistakenly look for the fictitious criminal law reports.

European Journal of Crime, Criminal Law and Criminal Justice. The Hague and London: Kluwer. ISSN: 0928-9569.

Journal of Criminal Law. Douglas, Isle of Man: Vathek. ISSN: 0022-0183 (JCL).

Available on *LexisNexis Professional.*

Journal of Financial Crime: The Official Journal of the Cambridge International Symposium on Economic Crime. London: Henry Stewart. ISSN: 1359-0790.

Journal of International Criminal Justice. Oxford: Oxford University Press. ISSN: 1478-1387 (JICJ).

New academic journal covering international criminal justice and looking at the law, jurisprudence, criminology and the history of international institutions.

Online services

Crime Online

Part of *Butterworths LexisNexis Direct Services*, this database includes 6,000 cases, statutes, statutory instruments, practice directions and the full text of *Blackstone's Criminal Practice.*

Criminal Appeal Reports and Sentencing *(The Justis Databases)*

Stone's Justices' Manual Direct

Part of *Butterworths LexisNexis Direct Services*, the online version of the manual includes *The Directory of UK Magistrates' Courts* as well as links to criminal reports in *The All England Law Reports* and unreported transcripts.

Websites

CJS Online (Criminal Justice System Website) (*http://www.cjsonline.org/home.html*)

The *CJS Online* site brings all the criminal justice agencies together and is split into an area for practitioners and a separate part for citizens.

Criminal Cases Review Commission (*http://www.ccrc.gov.uk*)

The site for this organisation, which reviews suspected miscarriages of criminal justice, has annual reports, publications, press releases and an online application form.

Criminal Courts Review (*http://www.criminal-courts-review.org.uk*)

Has the full report and a summary of Lord Justice Auld's *Review of the Criminal Courts System*, published in September 2001.

Criminal Law Week Online (*http://www.criminal-law.co.uk*)

Aimed at practitioners, this subscription site has a weekly digest of developments in criminal law. There is also a print version available and a choice of subscriptions to have the print or Internet version or both.

The Crown Prosecution Service (*http://www.cps.gov.uk*)

The site for the CPS site has press releases, policy statements, the code for prosecutors and CPS instructions for prosecutor advocates.

Harassment Law (*http://www.harassment-law.co.uk*)

Run by barrister Neil Addison, this site has practical information and links for anyone who is a victim of harassment or is wrongly accused. This covers racial and sexual harassment, bullying at work and anti-social behaviour. There is an explanation of the Protection from Harassment Act 1997.

Home Office Legislation (*http://www.homeoffice.gov.uk/inside/legis/index.html*)

The legislation section of *Inside the Home Office* covers Home Office Acts, Bills currently before Parliament and statutory instruments. The Acts themselves are links to the HMSO site, but more interesting is the background information on the legislation, including Home Office research, available as pdf files.

The Lord Chancellor's Department: Criminal Matters (*http://www.lcd.gov.uk/criminal/crimfr.htm*)

Has links to official information sources, including the *Auld Review*.

Police Law (*http://www.policelaw.co.uk*)

Covers British criminal law for police, solicitors and users and has links to the details of relevant books and to Acts on official sites. Includes Home Office circulars and has a list of British police forces.

Scottish Criminal Cases Review Commission (*http://www.sccrc.co.uk*)

Has reports, news and court opinions on cases referred by the Commission. There are also example case studies providing details of the type of cases dealt with by the body.

UK Criminal Justice Web Links (*http://www.leeds.ac.uk/law/ccjs/ukweb-2.htm*)

Has a useful list of sites relating to the police and other agencies with comments. There are separate smaller lists for Europe, North America and the rest of the world.

18

Civil procedure and the courts

There have been massive changes to the civil justice system, with the Civil Procedure Rules 1998 revolutionising the way people make civil claims and the way the courts deal with them. Since the rules were introduced, there have been many amendments, including the Civil Procedure Amendment Rules 2002.

Books

Atkins, James Richard. *Atkin's Encyclopaedia of Court Forms in Civil Proceedings* (2nd edn). London: Butterworths. ISBN: 040601020X (for set). (Court Forms (2nd edn)).

Subscription set with a consolidated index and supplements.

Blackstone's Civil Practice. Oxford: Oxford University Press.

With CD-Rom. Also available as *Blackstone's Civil Practice Online* (see p. 132).

This massive annual sets out the course of proceedings from pre-action protocols to enforcement of judgments. A look at the litigation process in general is followed by chapters on topics frequently considered by the county courts, including landlord and tenant and consumer credit. There is a useful section summarising the changes in terminology since the Civil Procedure Rules.

Butt, Peter and Castle, Richard. *Modern Legal Drafting: A Guide to Using Clearer Language.* Cambridge: Cambridge University Press, 2001. xxvi, 181p. ISBN: 0521001862.

The Civil Court Practice. London: Butterworths.

Annual, with supplements, which covers the jurisdiction and procedure of the civil courts and is also known as *The Green Book*. The three sections of the work over two volumes cover rules and procedure, general jurisdiction of the courts, and special powers and procedures under particular statutes.

Civil Court Service. Bristol: Jordans.

The Brown Book by Lord Justice Laws, Richard Stevens and Bill Vincent, this is an alternative to *The White Book* and *The Green Book*, namely *Civil Procedure* (The White Book Service) and *The Civil Court Practice*. There is a newsletter issued with it and a full copy of the book and extra up-to-date statutes are included in the accompanying CD-Rom.

It is soon to be launched as an online service as well (see *http://www .lawreportsonline.co.uk* for details). This will have additional statutory material and an archive of the *Civil Court Service Newsletter*.

Civil Procedure (The White Book Service). London: Sweet & Maxwell.

With general editor Lord Justice May, this is *The White Book* covering County Court and High Court procedure. Supplements and a newsletter support the current volumes. A new A4 forms volume has versions for photocopying of all the forms needed under the civil justice regime. There is also a CD-Rom with the forms in pdf and rtf, so they can be edited for use.

The White Book is also available on *Westlaw*.

Dennis, Ian. *The Law of Evidence* (2nd edn). London: Sweet & Maxwell, 2002. lvi, 757p. ISBN: 0421742003.

Encyclopaedia of Forms and Precedents (5th edn). London: Butterworths. ISBN: 0406023603 (set) (Forms & Precedents (5th edn)).

Subscription with replacement volumes, consolidated index and form finder. Also available on *Butterworths LexisNexis Direct Services*.

Foster, Charles, Popat, Prashant and Gilliatt, Jacqueline. *Civil Advocacy: A Practical Guide* (2nd edn). London: Cavendish, 2001. 186p. ISBN: 1859415628.

Guide to practice and procedure in courts and tribunals.

Fridd, Nicholas. *Basic Practice in Court, Tribunals and Inquiries* (3rd edn). London: Sweet & Maxwell, 2000. xii, 384p. ISBN: 0421684801.

Griffith, J.A.G. *The Politics of the Judiciary* (5th edn). London: Fontana, 1997. xxvii, 376p. ISBN: 0006863817.

Howard, M.N. (gen. ed.). *Phipson on Evidence* (15th edn, The Common Law Library). London: Sweet & Maxwell, 2000. cclxxii, 1,634p. ISBN: 0421616806.

Updated by supplements.

Huxley, Phil, & O'Connell, Michael. *Blackstone's Statutes on Evidence.* London: Blackstone Press.

Annual.

Jacob, I.H. *Chitty and Jacob's Queen's Bench Forms.* (21st edn, The Common Law Library). London: Sweet & Maxwell, 1986. xlv, 1,709p. ISBN: 0421206004.

A library of precedents. Kept up to date by cumulative supplements.

Jacob, Joseph M. *Civil Litigation: Practice and Procedure in a Shifting Culture.* Welwyn Garden City: EMIS Publishing, 2001. xi, 155p. ISBN: 1858112486.

Keane, Adrian. *The Modern Law of Evidence* (5th edn). London: Butterworths, 2000. cvii, 686p. ISBN: 0406921822.

The Legal Services Commission Manual. London: Sweet & Maxwell. Loose-leaf. ISBN: Vol. 1 – 0421728701; Vol. 2 – 0421728809; Vol. 3 – 0421728906; Vol. 4 – 0421729007.

This is the official guide to the public funding scheme and consists of up to four volumes. The subscription is flexible, so the volumes relevant to your kind of practice, civil or criminal, may be chosen. There is an additional CD-Rom.

Marshall, Enid A. *Gill: The Law of Arbitration* (4th edn). London: Sweet & Maxwell, 2001. xx, 206p. ISBN: 0421681306.

Murphy, Peter (ed.). *Evidence, Proof and Facts.* Oxford: Oxford University Press, 2003. xiv, 602p. ISBN: 0199261954.

Sourcebook of extracts of important primary and secondary sources in the field of evidence, proof and facts. Includes such issues as logic and rhetoric in the context of judicial proof, the place of different kinds of probability theory in legal proof and the role of causation in legal proof.

Murphy, Peter. *Murphy on Evidence* (7th edn). London: Blackstone Press, 2000. lxiv, 605p. ISBN: 1841740209.

O'Hare, John and Browne, Kevin. *Civil Litigation* (10th edn, Litigation Library). London: Sweet & Maxwell, 2001. lxxxii, 849p. ISBN: 0421826509.

Pearl, Patricia. *Small Claims Procedure: A Practical Guide* (2nd edn, Civil Litigation in Practice). Welwyn Garden City: CLT Professional, 2000. xvi, 284p. ISBN: 1858112206.

Peysner, John (gen. ed.). *Civil Litigation Handbook.* London: Law Society, 2001. xxvii, 559p. ISBN: 1853285927.

Prime, Terence and Scanlan, Gary. *The Law of Limitation* (2nd edn). Oxford: Oxford University Press, 2001. xxxix, 423p. ISBN: 1841741868.

New edition of *The Modern Law of Limitation.* 2001, which was mentioned in Law Commission reports looking at reform in this area. This new edition examines the impact of limitation on civil litigation and the individual periods of limitation under the Limitation Act 1980 in relation to specific causes of action.

Pyke, James. *A–Z of Civil Litigation.* London: Sweet & Maxwell, 2001. 975p. ISBN: 0752006088.

Pyke, James and Oldham, Dave. *Practical Civil Court Precedents*. London: Sweet & Maxwell. Loose-leaf. ISBN: 0851218989.

Rose, William M. *Pleadings Without Tears: A Guide to Legal Drafting under the Civil Procedure Rules* (6th edn). Oxford: Oxford University Press, 2002. x, 349p. ISBN: 0199254389.

Legal drafting and the fundamental principles of successful pleadings in the light of the many changes introduced by the Civil Procedure Rules. Covers skeleton arguments. Has kept 'pleadings' in the title rather than the new 'statements of case'.

Sime, Stuart. *A Practical Approach to Civil Procedure* (5th edn). Oxford: Oxford University Press, 2002. lx, 548p. ISBN: 0199254370.

Covers the main areas of civil procedure, concentrating on the points most likely to arise in a day-to-day practice.

Thompson, P.K.J. and Di Mambro, Louise (gen. eds). *Butterworths Civil Court Precedents*. London: Butterworths. ISBN: 0406985022.

Loose-leaf.

Watson, Brian. *Litigation Liabilities*. Bembridge: Palladian, 2002. lvii, 613p. ISBN: 1902558529.

Law reports

Civil Practice Law Reports. Birmingham: CLT Professional. ISSN: 1465-7414.

Journals

Civil Justice Quarterly. London: Sweet & Maxwell. ISSN: 0261-9261.

Online services

Civil Procedure Online

Part of *Butterworths LexisNexis Direct Services*. Has full-text of *The Civil Court Practice (The Green Book)*.

Civil Procedure Rules *(The Justis Databases)*

Added to the service in October 2002.

Encyclopaedia of Forms and Precedents

An alternative to the print subscription and part of *Butterworths LexisNexis Direct Services*.

Everyform *(http://www.everyform.net)*

Part of *Butterworths LexisNexis Direct Services*, this supplies online forms for solicitors. There are three levels of service to choose from, including a simple free service.

Lawtel Civil Procedure

Lawtel includes a section devoted to civil procedure and also has *Blackstone's Civil Practice Online*.

Websites

Access to Justice Final Report *(http://www.law.warwick.ac.uk/woolf/report/)*

The Warwick University site has the full text of the report on civil justice reforms, *Access to Justice*, by Lord Woolf.

Court Service Web Site (*http://www.courtservice.gov.uk*)

The site of the Executive Agency of the Lord Chancellor's Department has daily court listings, court addresses, statutory forms, practice directions and a selection of judgments chosen by the judge concerned. The site has been revamped with a new feel and navigation system and is now divided into three main sections covering using the courts, legal and professional, and a section about the Court Service.

Legal Services Commission (*www.legalservices.gov.uk*)

The site for the successor to the Legal Aid Board includes information for the public, news and links to relevant statutory material.

The Scottish Courts Web Site (*http://www.scotcourts.gov.uk*)

Site sponsored by the Scottish Court Service covers all civil and criminal courts in Scotland. Has location and telephone numbers of the courts and details of recent judgments which can be searched for. In addition, the site has information on some parts of the Scottish Executive Justice Department.

Scottish Legal Aid Board On-line (*www.slab.org.uk*)

The Scottish equivalent of the Legal Services Commission has information for the public and legal profession.

19

Family law

Family law is in flux, with pressures for it to change and adapt with the Human Rights Act 1998 having the potential to bring changes across the board. *White v. White* (2000) was the most important case on financial settlement on divorce for thirty years, the House of Lord's decision causing a major upheaval of ancillary relief. The Children Act 1989 is still very important for children's law and the Adoption and Children Act was passed in 2002. Marriage law was affected by the Divorce (Religious Marriages) Act 2002.

Books

Aquino, Tracey. *Family Law* (4th edn, Cavendish Q and A Series). London: Cavendish, 2003. 340p. ISBN: 185941737X.

Bird, Roger. *Ancillary Relief Handbook* (3rd edn). Bristol: Family Law, 2002. xxxvii, 399p. ISBN: 0853087393.

Bird, Roger. *Child Support: The New Law* (5th edn). Bristol: Family Law, 2002. xxiv, 314p. ISBN: 085308761X.

Bird, Roger. *Domestic Violence and Protection from Harassment* (3rd edn). London: Family Law, 2001. xxiv, 220p. ISBN: 0853086664.

New edition on the way (see publisher's website, *http://www.jordanpublishing.co.uk*).

Bird, Roger and Salter, David. *Family Law Precedents Service.* Bristol: Jordans. Loose-leaf. ISBN: 085308727X.

Annotated collection of precedents for applications and orders in family proceedings. With CD-Rom, which has the precedents, so they can be used and adapted.

Black, Jill M., Bridge, Jane and Bond, Tina. *A Practical Approach to Family Law* (6th edn). London: Blackstone Press, 2000. xlvi, 632p. ISBN: 1854318748.

Covers the reform of divorce law, the increasing use of mediation, changes to pension sharing and welfare benefits. It also deals with the radical changes introduced by the Children Act 1989 and looks at the Child Support Act 1991.

Blomfield, Robert and Brooks, Helen. *A Practical Guide to Family Proceedings* (2nd edn). Bristol: Family Law, 2002. xliii, 469p. ISBN: 0853087636.

Border, Rosy and Muir, Jane. *Divorce.* London: Cavendish, 2001. 251p. ISBN: 185941818X.

Covers all aspects of divorce law, including mediation, children and dealing with domestic violence.

Burrows, David. *Ancillary Relief: The New Rules.* Bristol: Family Law, 2000. 416p. ISBN: 0853085257.

Burton, Frances. *Family Law.* London: Cavendish, 2003. lxviii, 520p. ISBN: 1859414710.

Covers the main topics in respect of children, marriage, unmarried couples, divorce and domestic violence. Includes changes to ancillary relief in the wake of *White* v. *White*, the implications of the Human Rights Act and the Adoption and Children Act 2002.

Butterworths Family Law Service. London: Butterworths. Loose-leaf. ISBN: 040610719X.

Butterworths Family Law and Child Law Bulletin comes with the subscription.
Also available on CD-Rom as part of *Butterworths Family and Child Law Library* and as part of the online service *Family and Child Law Direct* (see p. 141).

Cleland, Alison and Sutherland, Elaine E. (eds). *Children's Rights in Scotland.* Edinburgh: W. Green, 2001. xxxiv, 368p. ISBN: 0414013492.

Cracknell, D.G. *Family Law* (3rd edn, Cracknell's Statutes). London: Old Bailey Press. xiii, 444p. ISBN: 185836471X.

Cretney, Stephen M. *Family Law* (4th edn, Sweet & Maxwell's Textbook Series). London: Sweet & Maxwell, 2000. l, 376p. ISBN: 0421669802.

Cretney, Stephen M. (ed.). *Family Law: Essays for the New Millennium.* Bristol: Family Law, 2000. 201p. ISBN: 0853086656.

Cretney, Stephen M., Masson, Judith and Bailey-Harris, Rebecca. *Principles of Family Law* (7th edn). London: Sweet & Maxwell, 2003. cxix, 901p. ISBN: 0421717602.

Covers the impact of the Family Law Act 1996 and the European Convention on Human Rights.

The Family Court Practice. Bristol: Family Law. ISBN: 0853088640 (2003 hardback and CD-Rom).

A subscription available in print and CD-Rom versions.

Goff, Robert and Jones, Gareth. *Law of Restitution.* London: Sweet & Maxwell, 2002. 436p. ISBN: 042182820X.

Gumbel, Elizabeth-Anne, Johnson, Malcolm and Scorer, Richard. *Child Abuse Compensation Claims: A Practitioner's Guide.* London: Law Society, 2002. xxvi, 262p. ISBN: 1853287172.

Hall, Sir William Clarke and Morrison, Arthur Cecil Lockwood. *Clarke Hall and Morrison on Children.* London: Butterworths. Loose-leaf. ISBN: 040996628.

Also available on CD-Rom as part of *Butterworths Family and Child Law Library* and as part of the online service *Family and Child Law Direct* (see p. 141).

Hayward Smith, Rodger and Newton, Clive R. Jackson's Matrimonial Finance and Taxation (7th edn). London: Butterworths, 2002. xcviii, 1,054p. ISBN: 0406941491.

Also included on CD-Rom as part of *Butterworths Family and Child Law Library* and as part of the online service *Family and Child Law Direct* (see p. 141).

Herring, Jonathan (ed.). *Family Law: Issues, Debates, Policy.* Cullompton: Willan, 2001. xvii, 237p. ISBN: 1903240190.

Covers adoption and children generally and domestic violence as well as divorce and family property. Considers the implications of the Human Rights Act and looks at policy issues and proposals for reform.

Hershman, David and McFarlane, Andrew (eds). *Hershman and McFarlane Children Act Handbook 2002.* Bristol: Family Law, 2002. vii, 419p. ISBN: 0853087989.

Key legislation and guidance relating to proceedings under the Children Act 1989. A consolidated, fully amended and annotated version of the Act is included, as are relevant sections from other statutes.

Law Society. *Family Law Protocol.* London: Law Society, 2002. xv, 112p. ISBN: 1853288853.

Sets out the Law Society's best practice for solicitors in England and Wales to comply with the Society's rules on family law.

Lyon, Christina. *Child Abuse* (3rd edn). Bristol: Family Law, 2003. lxxvi, 736p. ISBN: 0853085765.

The protection of children from abuse, covering civil and criminal proceedings. Updated to cover new legislation, including the Human Rights Act and the Children (Leaving Care) Act 2000. Looks at several inquiries into failures of the child protection scheme.

Mitchell, John. *Children Act Private Law Proceedings: A Handbook*. Bristol: Family Law, 2003. liv, 458p. ISBN: 0853088071.

Child disputes, such as paternity and parental responsibility, in the light of the welfare principles underpinning the Act and in the wake of new technologies, such as assisted fertilisation.

Mostyn, Nicholas and Nicolson, John. *Ancillary Relief: A Guide to the New Rules*. London: Butterworths, 2000. 106p. ISBN: 040693178X.

Oldham, Mika (ed.). *Blackstone's Statutes on Family Law*. Oxford: Oxford University Press.

Annual.

Pearson, Philippa. *Do-It-Yourself Cohabitation Rights*. London: Law Pack Publishing, 2001. 86p. ISBN: 1902646525.

Rayden, William and Jackson, Joseph. *Rayden and Jackson's Law and Practice in Divorce and Family Matters* (17th edn). London: Butterworths, 1997. 3v. ISBN: 0406890404 (set).

A loose-leaf service volume accompanies two hard-copy volumes.

Also available on CD-Rom as part of *Butterworths Family and Child Law Library* and as part of the online service *Family and Child Law Direct* (see p. 141).

Standley, Kate. *Family Law* (3rd edn, Palgrave Law Masters). Basingstoke: Palgrave, 2001. lviii, 395p. ISBN: 0333949420.

Swindells, Heather et al. *Family Law and the Human Rights Act 1998*. Bristol: Family Law, 1999. l, 488p. ISBN: 0853085730.

White, Richard, Carr, Paul and Lowe, Nigel. *The Children Act in Practice* (3rd edn). London: Butterworths, 2002. lxiv, 747p. ISBN: 0406940037.

Revised to take into account new statutory and case law developments relating to the Children Act 1989, said by the authors to be the most important reform of child law in the twentieth century. Includes the text of the Act as now amended, with annotations and more in-depth commentary on how it operates in practice.

Law reports

Butterworths Family Court Reporter. London: Butterworths. ISSN: 0952-8199.

Family Law Reports. Bristol: Jordans. ISSN: 0261-4375 (FLR).
Also available as *Family Law Reports Online* (see p. 141).

Journals

Family Law. Bristol: Jordans. ISSN: 0014-7281 (Fam Law).

Family Law Bulletin. London: Sweet & Maxwell. ISSN: 1472-2054.

Online services

Butterworths Family and Child Law Library
This CD-Rom service has information from core works on family law by Butterworths, including *Butterworths Family Law Service, Rayden and Jackson, Clarke Hall and Morrison* and *Jackson's Matrimonial Finance and Taxation*.

Family and Child Law Direct

Part of *Butterworths LexisNexis Direct Services*, this online service has similar coverage to *Butterworths Family and Child Law Library*.

Family Law Reports (The Justis Databases)

Family Law Reports Online (FLR Online)

Part of Jordans' service *LawReports Online* and includes the reports since they began in 1980. New parts are included before they appear in print and transcripts of key cases are also posted.

Websites

Family Law (*http://www.familylaw.co.uk/flhome.nsf/*)

An imprint of Jordan Publishing, the site has details of publications and online services.

Family Law Consortium (*http://www.tflc.co.uk*)

Formed in 1995, the Consortium brings together solicitors, mediators and counsellors. The site has useful information and articles on divorce, marriage and family law. It covers post-White cases.

20

Contract law

Civil liability, which has traditionally been based on case law, is increasingly affected by specialist legislation.

Major changes include the Unfair Terms and Consumer Contracts Regulations 1999 and the Contracts (Rights of Third Parties) Act 1999 as well as the case *Alfred McAlpine Construction Ltd* v. *Panatown Ltd*, which was concerned with the recovery of substantial damages for loss suffered by a third party. Internet contracting is a further development and the Electronic Communications Act 2000 and the Consumer Protection (Distance Selling) Regulations 2000 implemented European directives in this area.

Books

Atiyah, P.S. and Smith, Stephen A. *Introduction to the Law of Contract* (5th edn, Clarendon Law Series). Oxford: Clarendon Press, 1995. 479p. ISBN: 0198259522.

Sixth edition to be published (see publisher's website *http://www.oup.co.uk*).

Beale, H.G. (ed.). *Chitty on Contracts* (28th edn). London: Sweet & Maxwell, 1999. 2v. ISBN: 0421691905 – Vol. 1; 0421692405 – Vol. 2.

Beale, H.G., Bishop, W.D. and Furmston, M.P. *Contract Cases and Materials* (4th edn). London: Butterworths, 2001. lviii, 1,256p. ISBN: 040692404X.

Beatson, Jack. *Anson's Law of Contract* (28th edn). Oxford: Oxford University Press, 2002. xcv, 739p. ISBN: 0198765762.

Updated edition of the well-established work, covering new legislation, including the Contracts (Rights of Third Parties) Act 1999. Looks at European law and international conventions where they affect English law. Considers the wider concept of obligations and the overlap between contract and tort.

Cooke, P. J. and Oughton, David. *The Common Law of Obligations* (3rd edn). London: Butterworths, 2000. lviii, 676p. ISBN: 0406904146.

Cracknell, D.G. *Contract Law* (11th edn, Cracknell's Companion. Cases and Statutes). London: Old Bailey Press, 2000. vii, 367p. ISBN: 185836275X.

Furmston, M.P. *Cheshire, Fifoot and Furmston's Law of Contract* (14th edn). London: Butterworths, 2001. lxi, 762p. ISBN: 0406930589.

Updated to include the impact of the Contracts (Rights of Third Parties) Act.

Halson, Roger. *Contract Law.* Harlow: Longman, 2001. 538p. ISBN: 0582086477.

Harris, Donald, Campbell, David and Halson, Roger. *Remedies in Contract and Tort* (2nd edn, Law in Context). London: Butterworths, 2002. xlviii, 634p. ISBN: 0406904103.

Hedley, Steve. *A Critical Introduction to Restitution.* London: Butterworths, 2001. xxxii, 368p. ISBN: 0406932417.

Krishnan, Vickneswaren. *Obligations: Contract Law Textbook* (2nd edn). London: Old Bailey Press, 2000. xxxi, 416p. ISBN: 1858363675.

McKendrick, Ewan. *Contract Law* (4th edn, Palgrave Law Masters). Basingstoke: Palgrave, 2000. xli, 462p. ISBN: 0333461096.

Poole, Jill. *Casebook on Contract* (5th edn). London: Blackstone Press, 2001. xxxvi, 751p. ISBN: 1841742171.

As a companion to the author's *Textbook on Contract*, this casebook is designed for undergraduate courses and has been updated to include recent decisions, including those on remedies for misrepresentation.

Poole, Jill. *Textbook on Contract* (6th edn). London: Blackstone Press, 2001. xxxvi, 513p. ISBN: 1841741949.

Updated to include the new legislation on Internet contracting. Links with the text in the author's *Casebook on Contract*.

Rose, Francis (ed.). *Blackstone's Statutes on Contract, Tort and Restitution.* Oxford: Oxford University Press.

Very useful source of statutes and statutory instruments. Includes European Union legislation. Annual.

Samuel, Geoffrey. *Law of Obligations and Legal Remedies* (2nd edn). London: Cavendish, 2001. lvi, 587p. ISBN: 1859415660.

Looks at obligations as a conceptual category, emphasising the special characteristics of the common law.

Samuel, Geoffery. *Sourcebook on Obligations and Legal Remedies* (2nd edn). London: Cavendish, 2000. lxxvi, 873p. ISBN: 1859415229.

Compilation of materials on obligations, concentrating on methodology and reasoning.

Smith, John Cyril. *The Law of Contract* (4th edn). London: Sweet & Maxwell, 2002. xxiv, 274p. ISBN: 042178170X.

Smith, John Cyril. *Smith and Thomas: A Casebook on Contract* (11th edn). London: Sweet & Maxwell, 2000. xxxv, 754p. ISBN: 0421716908.

Stone, Richard. *The Modern Law of Contract.* London: Cavendish, 2002. xli, 503p. ISBN: 1859416675.

Builds on the previous *Principles of Contract Law*, analysing case and statute law, using economic, empirical and sociological approaches. Also considers European law, including recent directives on electronic and distance contracts and the Lando Commission proposals for a European law of contract.

Treitel, G.H. *The Law of Contract* (10th edn). London: Sweet & Maxwell, 1999. xcv, 1,015p. ISBN: 042163460X.

Treitel, G.H. *Some Landmarks of Twentieth Century Contract Law.* Oxford: Clarendon Press, 2002. xix, 141p. ISBN: 019925575X.

21

Tort

Tort is a legal area that can make newspaper headlines with privacy cases and such disasters as Hillsborough. This section covers general works on tort and also material on negligence and personal injury. Negligence has faced upheaval with several House of Lords' decisions affecting professional negligence, and personal injury has developed into a separate specialism.

Books

Barrie, Peter. *Compensation for Personal Injuries.* London: Blackstone Press, 2002. xlvi, 905p. ISBN: 1841742864.

A book devoted to personal injury law which is increasingly becoming a self-contained specialist area. The relevant cases, statutes and practice directions are covered. The author is maintaining a website to keep up with developments in the law.

Dugdale, Anthony M. (gen. ed.). *Clerk and Lindsell on Torts* (18th edn). London: Sweet & Maxwell, 2000. ccxcvi, 1,863p. ISBN: 0421693401.

Updated by supplements.

Elliott, Catherine and Quinn, Frances. *Tort Law* (2nd edn). Harlow: Longman, 1999. xxii, 273p. ISBN: 0582381126.

Covers the full range of torts, including employer's liability, defamation, vicarious liability and deceit.

Exall, Gordon. *Personal Injury Litigation* (3rd edn, Cavendish Practice Notes). London: Cavendish, 2000. 179p. ISBN: 1859415776.

Gerven, Walter van, Lever, Jeremy and Larouche, Pierre. *Tort Law* (Common Law of Europe Casebooks). Oxford: Hart, 2000. xcix, 969p. ISBN: 1841131393.

Has cases and text on national and international tort law.

Giliker, Paula and Beckwith, Silas. *Tort* (Sweet & Maxwell's Textbook Series). London: Sweet & Maxwell, 2001. 392p. ISBN: 0421717009.

Harpwood, Vivienne. *Principles of Tort Law* (4th edn). London: Cavendish, 2000. 588p. ISBN: 1859414672.

Covers the range of tort law, including duty of care, breach of duty, occupiers' liability and quantum. Looks at the implications of the Human Rights Act and the Civil Procedure Rules in this area.

Fifth edition to be published (see publisher's website *http://www .cavendishpublishing.com*).

Harvey, Barbara and Marston, John. *Cases and Commentary on Tort* (4th edn). Harlow: Longman, 2000. xxxvi, 587p. ISBN: 0582423511.

Hepple, B.A., Howarth, David and Matthews, M.H. *Tort Cases and Materials* (5th edn). London: Butterworths, 2000. 1,151p. ISBN: 0406063265.

Hodgin, Ray (ed.). *Professional Liability: Law and Insurance* (2nd edn, Lloyd's Commercial Law Library). London: LLP, 1999. lxviii, 751p. ISBN: 1859786987.

Looks at the state of the law for professional liability for a range of different professions, including architects and engineers, auctioneers, accountants and auditors, estate agents, insurance intermediaries, solicitors and medical practice.

Jackson, Rupert M. and Powell, John L. *Jackson and Powell on Professional Negligence* (5th edn, The Common Law Library). London: Sweet & Maxwell, 2002. clxxvii, 1,320p. ISBN: 0421826002.

Jones, Michael A. *Textbook on Torts* (8th edn). London: Blackstone Press, 2002. lv, 727p. ISBN: 0199255334.

Comments on the impact of the Human Rights Act on torts.

Kidner, Richard. *Casebook on Torts* (7th edn). Oxford: Oxford University Press, 2002. xxxiv, 499p. ISBN: 019925480X.

Lunney, Mark and Oliphant, Ken. *Tort Law: Text and Materials*. Oxford: Oxford University Press, 2000. lvi, 819p. ISBN: 0198764014.

McBride, Nicholas J. and Bagshaw, Roderick. *Tort Law*. Harlow: Longman, 2001. lviii, 707p. ISBN: 0582257012.

Maddison, David, Tetlow, Christopher and Wood, Graham N. *Bingham's Negligence Cases* (5th edn). London: Sweet & Maxwell, 2002. 800p. ISBN: 042177830X.

Malcolm, Rosalind and Pointing, John. *Statutory Nuisance: Law and Practice*. Oxford: Oxford University Press, 2002. xlvii, 386p. ISBN: 0199242461.

Mullis, Alastair and Oliphant, Ken. *Torts* (3rd edn, Palgrave Law Masters). Basingstoke: Palgrave Macmillan, 2003. xxxiv, 422p. ISBN: 0333963792.

Covers the impact of the Human Rights Act and the Consumer Protection Act 1987 and recent developments relating to defamation, privacy, vicarious liability and the calculation of damages.

Solomon, Nicola, Middleton, Simon and Pritchard, John. *Personal Injury Litigation* (10th edn). London: Sweet & Maxwell, 2002. xxix, 693p. ISBN: 0752004417.

Walton, C.T. and Cooper, Roger, Ward, Simon E. (consultant ed.). *Charlesworth and Percy on Negligence* (10th edn, The Common Law Library, no. 6). London: Sweet & Maxwell, 2001. ccxlviii, 1,068p. ISBN: 0421825901.

Has supplement.

Weir, Tony. *A Casebook on Tort* (9th edn). London: Sweet & Maxwell, 2000. xxxix, 685p. ISBN: 0421689900.

Weir, Tony. *Tort Law* (Clarendon Law Series). Oxford: Oxford University Press, 2002. xxiv, 216p. ISBN: 0199249989.

Law reports

Professional Negligence and Liability Reports. London: Sweet & Maxwell. ISSN: 1363-4577 (PNLR).

From 1996 onwards, with a supplement covering key cases only from 1955 to 1995.

Journals

Journal of Personal Injury Law. London: Sweet & Maxwell. ISSN: 1352-7533.

Four issues a year. Previously *Journal of Personal Injury Litigation.*

Professional Negligence: A Journal of Liability, Ethics and Discipline. London: Cass. ISSN: 0267-078X.

Online services

Lawtel Personal Injury

Part of *Lawtel*, this includes personal injury quantum reports.

PI Online

Covers personal injury law and is part of *Butterworths LexisNexis Direct Services.*

Websites

Association of Personal Injury Lawyers (http://www.apil.com)

This is the website of the Nottingham-based association, which promotes the improvement of services provided to victims of accidents and clinical negligence.

Can I Claim?: The Accident Compensation Site (http://www.caniclaim.com)

The site provides online legal advice and information on making a claim for personal injury, medical or clinical negligence in England, Wales or Scotland. There is a free online assessment and then it is possible to contact a solicitor. The assessment panel consists of personal injury and medical negligence solicitors.

22

Equity and trusts

More than any other area, equity and trusts is heavily reliant on case law. However, there has been some important new legislation, in particular the Trustee Act 2000 but also the Trustee Delegation Act 1999, the Contracts (Rights of Third Parties) Act 1999 and the Child Support, Pension and Social Security Act 2000. The Law Commission has recently looked at trustee exemption clauses.

Books

Chalmers, James. *Trusts: Cases and Materials*. Edinburgh: W. Green, 2002. xxviii, 303p. ISBN: 0414013379.

Scottish trust law.

Dixon, Martin. *Equity and Trusts* (4th edn, Cavendish Q and A Series). London: Cavendish, 2003. 340p. ISBN: 1859417418.

Edwards, Richard and Stockwell, Nigel. *Trusts and Equity* (5th edn). Harlow: Longman, 2002. xxviii, 486p. ISBN: 0582438101.

Sixth edition by Richard Edwards to be published (see publisher's website *http://www.pearsoneduc.com*).

Hanbury, Harold Greville and Martin, Jill E. *Modern Equity* (16th edn). London: Sweet & Maxwell, 2001. xci, 937p. ISBN: 0421716800.

This edition covers new developments, including the effects of the Human Rights Act on equitable remedies and changes to procedure and terminology introduced by the Civil Procedure Rules.

Hartley, William M. *Declaration of Trust: A Draftsman's Handbook* (2nd edn). London: Sweet & Maxwell, 2001. xvi, 140p. ISBN: 0752006053.

Hayton, David J. *Hayton and Marshall: Commentary and Cases on the Law of Trusts and Equitable Remedies* (11th edn). London: Sweet & Maxwell, 2001. xciii, 1,079p. ISBN: 0421717807.

Combined textbook and casebook which deals with recent developments, including trustees' powers and duties under the Trustee Act 2000. Previous edition was published as: *Cases and Commentary on the Law of Trusts and Equitable Remedies*. 1996.

Hudson, Alastair. *Equity and Trusts* (2nd edn). London: Cavendish, 2001. 1,016p. ISBN: 1859414702.

Highlights the problems with the law of restitution and explores the commercial and welfare uses of trusts. A new edition is to be published (see publisher's website for details: *http://www.cavendishpubishing.com*).

Mowbray, John et al. *Lewin on Trusts* (17th edn, Property and Conveyancing Library). London: Sweet & Maxwell, 2000. ccxiv, 1,508p. ISBN: 0421233907.

Pearce, Robert and Stevens, John. *The Law of Trusts and Equitable Obligations* (3rd edn). London: Butterworths, 2002. lxi, 882p. ISBN: 0406946833.

Four years after the last edition, this work is updated to examine the law of trusts from a modern conceptual perspective, taking into account issues of current importance such as pension funds, unit trusts and the relationship between trusts and contracts.

Petit, Philip H. *Equity and the Law of Trusts* (9th edn). London: Butterworths, 2001. cxvii, 757p. ISBN: 0406937613.

Reed, P.J. and Wilson, R.C. *The Trustee Act 2000: A Practical Guide*. Bristol: Jordans, 2001. xix, 160p. ISBN: 0853086648.

Thurston, John. *A Practitioner's Guide to Trusts* (4th edn). Croydon: Tolley, 2002. xl, 301p. ISBN: 0754519996.

Todd, Paul and Watt, Gary. *Cases and Materials on Equity and Trusts* (4th edn). Oxford: Oxford University Press, 2003. xxxviii, 545p. ISBN: 019926192X.

This casebook complements the author's *Textbook on Trusts* and as well as covering the cases has the main statutory materials and extracts from journal articles.

Todd, Paul and Wilson, Sarah. *Textbook on Trusts* (6th edn). Oxford: Oxford University Press, 2003. xxvi, 498p. ISBN: 0199260737.

Tolley's Administration of Trusts. London: Tolley. Loose-leaf. ISBN: 0754516008.

Virgo, G.J. and Burn, E.H. (consultant ed.). *Maudsley and Burn's Trusts and Trustees: Cases and Materials* (6th edn). London: Butterworths, 2002. xcvi, 1,033p. ISBN: 0406985863.

Has cases and statutes and extracts from books, articles and reports on law reform linked by commentary and questions. Covers the increasing influence of restitution in respect of resulting trusts, constructive trusts and breach of trust and also looks at pension rights.

Websites

Charity Commission (*http://www.charity-commission.gov.uk*)

The official site for the Commission overseeing charities has a lot of useful information, including press releases, a list of registered charities and an A–Z list of links to official bodies relevant to this area. Moreover, the Commission's operational guidance is being added, with legal requirements and key procedures highlighted.

Public Guardianship Office (*http://www.guardianship.gov.uk*)

The site for the PGO, the administrative arm of the Court of Protection and the replacement of the Public Trust Office, has information about making an application to the court.

Trust Law Committee (*http://www.kcl.ac.uk/depsta/law/tlc*)

Chaired by Sir John Vinelott, the Committee was set up in 1994 by leading academics and practitioners to look at the weaknesses of trust law and is based at the School of Law, King's College, London. The site includes background on the Committee's work. Annual reports and the consultation papers can be downloaded as rtf or pdf files.

23

Property law

Always hard for students to come to grips with, land or property law is facing its biggest reform since 1925, with the Land Registration Act 2002 introducing major changes to residential and commercial conveyancing. This Act sets up the future large-scale and compulsory adoption of electronic conveyancing. The Law Commission has recently considered land valuation and housing tribunals.

Some books covering personal property are included.

Books

Abbey, Robert M. and Richards, Mark B. *Blackstone's Guide to the Land Registration Act 2002*. Oxford: Oxford University Press, 2002. xxiv, 249p. ISBN: 0199257965.

Covers the impact of the Act on residential and commercial conveyancing and Land Registry practice and looks at the future development of e-conveyancing. Includes a copy of the Act.

Abbey, Robert M. and Richards, Mark B. *A Practical Approach to Conveyancing* (4th edn). Oxford: Oxford University Press, 2002. xxxvi, 682p. ISBN: 0199254508.

Goes through the steps involved in conveyancing and advises on how to achieve an efficient and cost-effective service. Has precedent documents and examples of clauses and forms. Includes residential leasehold transactions.

Bray, Judith. *Land Law* (Key Facts). London: Hodder & Stoughton, 2002. v, 104p. ISBN: 0340845856.

Burn, E.H. *Cheshire and Burn's Modern Law of Real Property* (16th edn). London: Butterworths, 2000. 1,107p. ISBN: 0406983046.

Chappelle, Diane. *Land Law* (5th edn, The Foundation Studies in Law Series). Harlow: Longman, 2002. xxxi, 483p. ISBN: 0582438187.

The implication of changes to land registration is considered.

Clarke, Wayne (coordinating ed.). *Fisher and Lightwood's Law of Mortgage* (11th edn). London: Butterworths, 2002. clxxiv, 1,110p. ISBN: 0406999759.

Dixon, Martin. *Principles of Land Law* (4th edn, Cavendish Principles of Law Series). London: Cavendish, 2002. xlix, 442p. ISBN: 1859414729.

Considers the impact of the Land Registration Act 2002.

Gray, Kevin J. and Gray, Susan Francis. *Elements of Land Law* (3rd edn). London: Butterworths, 2001. cxxx, 1,502p. ISBN: 040698302X.

Gray, Kevin J. and Gray, Susan Francis. *Land Law* (2nd edn, Butterworths Core Text Series). London: Butterworths, 2001. xlvi, 544p. ISBN: 040694685X.

Covers modern land law, examining the increasing influence of environmental law, human rights law and European Union law.

Third edition to be published (see publisher's website *http://www.butterworths .co.uk*).

Green, Kate and Cursley, Joe. *Land Law* (4th edn, Palgrave Law Masters). Basingstoke: Palgrave, 2001. xviii, 222p. ISBN: 0333802942.

Harpum, Charles and Bignell, Janet. *Registered Land: The New Law: A Guide to The Land Registration Act 2002*. Bristol: Jordans, 2002. xxxvi, 335p. ISBN: 0853087598.

Lawson, F.H. and Ruden, Bernard. *The Law of Property* (3rd rev. edn, Clarendon Law Series). Oxford: Oxford University Press, 2002. ix, 206p. ISBN: 0198299931.

Wide-ranging, covering all aspects of property law, not just land law but also personal property and trusts. Includes the management of trusts, trusts of land and electronic conveyancing.

Megarry, Sir Robert. *A Manual of the Law of Real Property* (8th edn). London: Sweet & Maxwell, 2002. lxxix, 651p. ISBN: 0421717904.

Covers all major topics including the new Land Registration Act and Commonhold and Leasehold Reform Act 2002.

Megarry, Sir Robert and Wade, Sir William. *The Law of Real Property* (6th edn). London: Sweet & Maxwell, 2000. cxlix, 1,478p. ISBN: 042147470X.

Murphy, W.T. and Roberts, Simon. *Understanding Property Law* (3rd edn, Understanding Law). London: Sweet & Maxwell, 1998. xiii, 273p. ISBN: 0421634901.

Fourth edition to be published (see publisher's website: *http://www.smlawpub .co.uk*).

Panesar, Sukhinder. *General Principles of Property Law*. Harlow: Longman, 2001. xvi, 253p. ISBN: 0582423325.

Examines the fundamental principles of property law to help students gain a better understanding of a complex subject.

Property Law. London: Sweet & Maxwell.

Compiled from *Westlaw*, this includes up-to-date versions of statutes and statutory instruments, with any amendments included. Annual.

Riddall, John and Trevelyan, John. *Rights of Way: A Guide to Law and Practice* (3rd edn). Henley-on-Thames: Open Space Society, 2001. xxxv, 714p. ISBN: 1901184455.

Rook, Deborah. *Property Law and Human Rights* (Blackstone's Human Rights Series). London: Blackstone Press, 2001. xxvii, 394p. ISBN: 184174154X.

Silverman, Frances. *The Law Society's Conveyancing Handbook* (9th edn, 2002). London: Law Society, 2002. xlv, 1,201p. ISBN: 1853287423.

Practical guide to conveyancing, including recent developments such as electronic conveyancing.

Smith, Roger J. *Property Law* (4th edn, Longman Law Series). Harlow: Longman, 2003. lxviii, 617p. ISBN: 0582473241.

The established work has been updated to cover the recent changes in legislation and the important recent case law affecting estoppel remedies and undue influence in mortgages. The Human Rights Act is also considered.

Smith, Roger J. *Property Law: Cases and Materials* (2nd edn, Longman Law Series). Harlow: Longman, 2003. v, 836p. ISBN: 0582473381.

Companion volume to the textbook by the same author.

Stevens, John and Pearce, Robert. *Land Law* (2nd edn, Sweet & Maxwell's Textbook Series). London: Sweet & Maxwell, 2000. xlviii, 628p. ISBN: 0421690003.

Third edition to be published (see publisher's website *http://www.smlawpub.co.uk*).

Tee, Louise (ed.). *Land Law: Issues, Debates, Policy.* Cullompton: Willan, 2002. xix, 252p. ISBN: 190324076X.

Thomas, Meryl (ed.). *Blackstone's Statutes on Property Law.* Oxford: Oxford University Press.

Annual.

Worthington, Sarah. *Personal Property Law: Texts and Materials.* Oxford: Hart, 2000. xl, 716p. ISBN: 1901362442.

Law reports

Estates Gazette Law Reports. London: Estates Gazette. ISSN: 00951-9289 (EGLR).

Continues: *Estates Gazette Digest of Land and Property Cases.*
   Available on *LexisNexis Professional.*

Property, Planning and Compensation Reports. London: Sweet & Maxwell. ISSN: 0033-1295 (P&CR).

Covers mortgages, landlord and tenant, real property and town and country planning.

Journals

The Conveyancer and Property Lawyer. London: Sweet & Maxwell. ISSN: 0010-8200 (Conv).

Available on *Westlaw.*

Estates Gazette. London: Estates Gazette. ISSN: 0014-1240 (EG).

A mixture of property news and legal aspects.
   Available on *LexisNexis Professional.*

Online services

Commercial Property Law Digest

Part of *Butterworths LexisNexis Direct Services.*

Websites

Egi (Property Law Service) (*http://www.propertylaw.co.uk*)

From the Estates Gazette Group, this is a subscription-based news, research and information service for the commercial property market.

Land Law (*http://www.landlaw.org.uk*)

Has articles and notes on property law and links to legislation and to useful websites.

Land Registry (*http://www.landreg.gov.uk*)

Has information on the Registry and links to sections on electronic conveyancing and the relevant legislation, including the Land Registration Act.

Party Walls (*http://www.partywalls.com*)

This site has resources on party walls provided by Paul Chynoweth.

24

Landlord and tenant law

The Commonhold and Leasehold Reform Act 2002 brought important changes to landlord and tenant law by introducing new forms of property ownership.

Books

Arlidge, Trevor M. *Commonhold Law*. London: Sweet & Maxwell. ISBN: 0421758805 (loose-leaf).

New loose-leaf volume to cover this major development.

Barnes, Michael (gen. ed.) et al. *Hill and Redman's Law of Landlord and Tenant* (18th edn). London: Butterworths. Loose-leaf. ISBN: 0406998167.

Has useful supplements including one on the Commonhold and Leasehold Reform Act 2002.

Clarke, David. *Clarke on Commonhold: Law, Practice and Precedents*. Bristol: Jordans. Loose-leaf. ISBN: 085308775X.

With CD-Rom containing the precedents.

Driscoll, James, Williams, Del W. and Boston, Charles E.J. *Handbook of Residential Tenancies*. London: Sweet & Maxwell. Loose-leaf. ISBN: 0421703105.

Fetherstonhaugh, Guy, Peters, Edward and Sefton, Mark. *Commonhold: Law and Practice*. London: Butterworths. Loose-leaf. ISBN: 0406964440.

Garner, Simon and Frith, Alexandra. *Practical Approach to Landlord and Tenant* (3rd edn, A Practical Approach Series). Oxford: Oxford University Press, 2002. lxxiii, 630p. ISBN: 0199254254.

A guide to the principles of landlord and tenant, the book includes an analysis of the statutory codes applying to residential and business tenancies.

Kay, Robert. *The Landlord and Tenant Handbook: A Practical Guide to Letting and Renting Residential Property* (2nd edn, Fitzwarren Handbooks). Aylesbury: Fitzwarren, 2001. 120p. ISBN: 0952481286.

Lewison, Kim (gen. ed.). *Woodfall: Landlord and Tenant* (28th edn). London: Sweet & Maxwell. Loose-leaf. ISBN: 0421228202.

The loose-leaf subscription service is accompanied by a regular bulletin and includes the *Landlord and Tenant Reports* (see p. 165). Also available on CD-Rom.

Ross, Murray J. *Ross: Commercial Leases and Precedents* (5th edn). London: Butterworths. Loose-leaf. ISBN: 0406896194.

Accompanied by CD-Rom. Previous edition: *Drafting and Negotiating Commercial Leases*. 1994.

Smith, P.F. *The Law of Landlord and Tenant* (6th edn). London: Butterworths, 2002. lxxx, 608p. ISBN: 0406946795.

This is a new edition of *Evans and Smith: The Law of Landlord and Tenant*. 1996.

Wilkie, Margaret and Cole, Godfrey. *Landlord and Tenant Law* (4th edn). Basingstoke: Macmillan, 2000. xxxv, 262p. ISBN: 0333794281.

Law reports

Landlord and Tenant Reports. London: Sweet & Maxwell. ISSN: 1463-4473
(L&TR).
Part of the *Woodfall* loose-leaf service. Available on *Westlaw*.

Journals

Landlord and Tenant Review. London: Sweet & Maxwell. ISSN: 1365-8018.
Six issues a year, with a digest of cases and legislation and a practitioner's page.
   Available on *Westlaw*.

25

Intellectual property and media law

With the growth of trade and the transfer of information around the world, intellectual property is of increasing importance. New technological developments, including the Internet, digital recording technology and genetics, pose new challenges for the law to deal with. The Copyright, etc. and Trade Marks (Offences and Enforcement) Act was passed in 2002 and European Union directives were implemented with the Copyright and Rights in Databases Regulations 1997 and the Electronic Communications Act 2000.

Books

United Kingdom law

Bainbridge, David I. *Intellectual Property* (5th edn). Harlow: Longman, 2002. xlv, 710p. ISBN: 0582473144.

Includes biotechnological patents, the Registered Designs Regulations 2001 and European aspects of trade marks.

Bently, Lionel and Sherman, Brad. *Intellectual Property Law*. Oxford: Oxford University Press, 2001. lxxxiii, 1,051p. ISBN: 0198763433.

Covers the way intellectual property rights are acquired, infringed and exploited. Includes copyright, trade marks, passing off, patents and design and confidential information. Looks at international and European law.

Black, Trevor. *Intellectual Property in the Digital Era* (Special Report). London: Sweet & Maxwell, 2002. xiv, 136p. ISBN: 0421824107.

Christie, Andrew and Gare, Stephen (eds). *Blackstone's Statutes on Intellectual Property*. London: Blackstone Press.

Includes European Union directives. Annual.

Colston, Catherine. *Principles of Intellectual Property Law*. London: Cavendish, 1999. lxi, 482p. ISBN: 1859414656.

Cornish, W.R. *Intellectual Property: Patents, Copyright, Trade Marks and Allied Rights* (4th edn). London: Sweet & Maxwell, 1999. 817p. ISBN: 0421635304.

New edition due (see publisher's website: *http://www.smlawpub.co.uk*).

Crone, Tom. *Law and the Media* (4th edn). Oxford: Focal Press, 2001. 373p. ISBN: 024051629X.

Firth, Alison (ed.), **with Phillips, Jeremy.** *An Introduction to Intellectual Property Law*. London: Butterworths, 2001. xliv, 443p. ISBN: 0406997578.

Garnett, Kevin and Davies, Gillian. *Copinger and Skone James on Copyright: Including International Copyright with the Statutes, Orders, Conventions and Agreements Thereto Relating and Precedents and Court Forms, Also Related Forms of Protection* (14th edn). London: Sweet & Maxwell, 1999. ISBN: 0421589108.

Updated with supplement.

Kitchin, David et al. *Kerly's Law of Trade Marks and Trade Names* (13th edn). London: Sweet & Maxwell, 2001. cx, 1,600p. ISBN: 0421456108.

Laddie, Hugh, Prescott, Peter and Vitoria, Mary. *The Modern Law of Copyright and Designs*. London: Butterworths, 2000. 3v. ISBN: 0406903832.

Marett, Paul. *Information Law in Practice* (2nd edn). Aldershot: Ashgate, 2002. xxix, 230p. ISBN: 0566083906.

New edition of: *Information Law and Practice*.

Michaels, Amanda. *A Practical Guide to Trade Mark Law* (3rd edn). London: Sweet & Maxwell, 2001. 430p. ISBN: 0421747609.

Olsen, John R. and Maniatis, Spyros M. *Trade Marks, Trade Names, and Unfair Competition: World Law and Practice.* London: Sweet & Maxwell. Loose-leaf. ISBN: 0752002759.

Owen, Lynette. *Selling Rights* (4th edn). London: Routledge, 2001. xii, 308p. ISBN: 0415235081.

Practical guide to selling rights and co-publications worldwide. Has been updated to include changes in technology, particularly the Internet, sales and distribution and to legislation in Britain and overseas.

Phillips, Jeremy (consultant ed.). *Butterworths Intellectual Property Law Handbook* (5th edn). London: Butterworths, 2001. x, 1,723p. ISBN: 0406944105.

A new edition is to be published (see publisher's site for details: *http://www .butterworths.co.uk*).

Robertson, Geoffrey and Nicol, Andrew. *Media Law* (4th edn). London: Sweet & Maxwell, 2002. xxxviii, 908p. ISBN: 0752005197.

Spilsbury, Sallie. *Media Law.* London: Cavendish, 2000. xxxviii, 570p. ISBN: 185941530X.

Covers regulation of the media industry and how far it enjoys freedom of expression in the light of the Human Rights Act. Also goes through the elements of a typical media agreement.

Stamatoudi, Irini A. *Copyright and Multimedia Products: A Comparative Analysis* (Cambridge Studies in Intellectual Property Rights). Cambridge: Cambridge University Press, 2002. xv, 317p. ISBN: 0521808197.

Thorley, Simon et al. *Terrell on the Law of Patents* (15th edn). London: Sweet & Maxwell, 2000. xcvii, 1,066p. ISBN: 0421624701.

Tritton, Guy [with] Davis, Richard et al. *Intellectual Property in Europe* (2nd edn). London: Sweet & Maxwell, 2002. lxxxv, 1,112p. ISBN: 0421641509.

Wall, Raymond A. et al. *Copyright Made Easier* (3rd edn). London: Aslib, 2000. 548p. ISBN: 0851424473.

European law

Prime, Terence. *European Intellectual Property Law* (European Business Law Library). Aldershot: Ashgate, 2000. vii, 320p. ISBN: 1855215667.

Law reports

Butterworths Intellectual Property and Technology Cases. London: Butterworths.

Entertainment and Media Law Reports. Oxford: Sweet & Maxwell/ESC. ISSN: 0966-193X (EMLR).

Fleet Street Reports. London: Sweet & Maxwell. ISSN: 0141-9455 (FSR).
Has cases on intellectual property. Available on *Westlaw*.

Reports of Patent, Design and Trade Mark Cases. London: Sweet & Maxwell for Patent Office. ISSN: 0080-1364 (RPC).
Available on *Westlaw*.

Journals

Entertainment Law. London: Frank Cass. ISSN: 1473-0987.

European Intellectual Property Review. London: Sweet & Maxwell. ISSN: 0142-0461 (EIPR).

Available on *Westlaw*.

International Review of Industrial Property and Copyright Law. Munich: C.H. Beck [for] the Max Planck Institute for Foreign and International Patent, Copyright and Corporation Law. ISSN: 0018-9855 (IIC).

Yearbook of Copyright and Media Law. Oxford: Oxford University Press.

Has annual surveys of issues relating to copyright and entertainment and media law, covering British, European Union and international law.

Websites

AHRB Research Centre for Studies in Intellectual Property and Technology Law (*http://www.law.ed.ac.uk/ahrb/*)

The site for the centre of excellence for intellectual property law and information technology law, which is located in the School of Law, University of Edinburgh, has news on the activities of the centre and downloadable versions of publications and articles.

Copyright Licensing Agency (*http://www.cla.co.uk*)

The site for the non-profit-making agency which licenses organisations for photocopying and scanning has press and news releases and information on the implementation of the European copyright directive.

Copyright Website (*http://www.benedict.com*)

Site run by Benedict O'Mahoney on copyright has mainly American law, but it is interesting on the topic of copyright and the Internet.

Cyber Law Centre (*http://www.cyberlawcentre.org.uk*)

Useful site, if slightly hard to use, with links to Internet resources on intellectual property.

European Patent Office (*http://www.european-patent-office.org/index.htm*)

Has details of publications, news and links.

Intellectual Property (*http://www.intellectual-property.gov.uk*)

The site sponsored and maintained by the UK Patent Office covers British intellectual property on the Internet, with resources and links, latest news and notes explaining intellectual property.

The Intellectual Property Law Server (*http://www.intelproplaw.com*)

Covering intellectual property law worldwide, the site has news and articles and comprehensive links to copyright, patent and trade mark sites.

Jenkins (*http://www.jenkins-ip.com/patlaw*)

The law firm Jenkins has a guide to patents law, which covers legislation and European law.

UK Intellectual Property on the Internet (*http://www.intellectual-property .gov.uk*)

British government-backed site with links to relevant sites, latest news and answers to questions.

UK Patent Office (*http://www.patent.gov.uk*)

Has news and informative introductions to patents and trade marks. The site also makes available reference materials, such as forms.

26

Wills, probate and the administration of estates

This is not generally a contentious area, although there can be family disputes over estates. Many of the books are practical tools, with precedents included.

Books

Borkowski, Andrew. *Textbook on Succession* (2nd edn). Oxford: Oxford University Press, 2002. xxxiv, 393p. ISBN: 184174221X.

Academic book on the law of succession, which focuses on such important issues as the limits of testamentary freedom and the rights of spouses and children on intestacy. Includes the administration of estates.

Butler, John (contributing ed.). *Probate Practice Manual.* London: Sweet & Maxwell. Loose-leaf. ISBN: 0752002503.

Chatterton, David A. *Wills* (4th edn, Cavendish Practice Notes). London: Cavendish, 2001. ix, 112p. ISBN: 1859416632.

Updated to cover the Trusts of Land and Appointment of Trustees Act 1996, the Trustee Delegation Act 1999 and Trustee Act 2000.

D'Costa, Roland. *Executorship and Administration of Estates* (2nd edn, Cavendish Practice Notes). London: Cavendish, 2001. vii, 127p. ISBN: 1859414591.

Covers the powers, rights and duties of personal representatives responsible for handling an estate. Includes specimen forms and precedents and a glossary of terms.

Hiram, Hilary. *The Scots Law of Succession*. Edinburgh: Butterworths, 2002. xxx, 343p. ISBN: 040690040X.

Kerridge, R. (ed.). *Parry and Clark: The Law of Succession* (11th edn). London: Sweet & Maxwell, 2002. lxxxiii, 671p. ISBN: 0421741104.

Covers the Trustee Act 2000.

King, Lesley (gen. ed.). *Probate Practitioner's Handbook* (4th edn). London: Law Society, 2002. xv, 391p. ISBN: 1853288314.

Covers practice management and changes from the Trustee Act 2002 and the Financial Services and Markets Act 2000. Includes guidance on deaths abroad and unusual funerals.

MacDonald, D.R. *Succession* (3rd edn, Greens Concise Scots Law). Edinburgh: W. Green, 2001. xxxi, 228p. ISBN: 0414014367.

Scottish succession law.

Probate Plus **CD-ROM.** London: Sweet & Maxwell.

Tool for administration.

Ray, Ralph. *Wills and Post-Death Tax Planning: A Practical Approach* (3rd edn). Welwyn Garden City: EMIS Publishing, 2001. 182p. ISBN: 1858112869.

Ryan, Michael W.A. *A Practitioner's Guide to Executorship and Administration* (4th edn). Croydon: Tolley, 2000. 357p. ISBN: 0754507467.

Shenkman, Martin. *Estate Planning after the 2002 Tax Act: Guiding Your Clients Through the Changes* (Bloomberg Professional Library). Princeton, NJ: Bloomberg Press, 2002. xii, 304p. ISBN: 1576601218.

Tax aspects of estate planning.

Sherrin, C.H. et al. *Williams on Wills* (8th edn). London: Butterworths, 2002. 2v. ISBN: 0406933928 – Vol. 1; 0406933936 – Vol. 2.

Comes with computer disc, *Precedents on Disk*.

Sunnucks, James H.G. *Williams, Mortimer and Sunnucks: Executors, Administrators and Probate* (18th edn). London: Sweet & Maxwell, 2000. cxcvi, 1,383p. ISBN: 0421653302.

Winegarten, J.I., D'Costa, R. and Synak, T. *Tristram and Coote's Probate Practice* (29th edn). London: Butterworths, 2002. lxx, 1,186p. ISBN: 0406947201.

Covers both non-contentious and contentious probate. Forms included on disc.

Withers (firm) (editorial team). *Practical Will Precedents*. London: Sweet & Maxwell. Loose-leaf. ISBN: 0851213332.

Also available on CD-Rom.

Websites

Wills and Probate (*http://www.courtservice.gov.uk/you_courts/probate/index.htm*)

Part of the site by the Court Service has a guide to obtaining probate and to probate appointments and getting copies of probate records, and a directory of probate registry addresses.

27

Company and partnership law

The most important recent development has been the introduction of the limited liability partnership (LLP).

Books

Banks, R.C. L'Anson. *Lindley and Banks on Partnership* (18th edn). London: Sweet & Maxwell, 2002. clxi, 1,131p. ISBN: 0421673907.

Blackett-Ord, Mark. *Partnership: The Modern Law of Partnership, Limited Partnership and Limited Liability Partnership* (2nd edn). London: Butterworths, 2002. cv, 779p. ISBN: 0406946442.

Bourne, Nicholas. *Essential Company Law* (3rd edn, Cavendish Publishing Essential Law Series). London: Cavendish, 2000. 123p. ISBN: 1859416055.

Boyle, John et al. (eds). *Boyle and Birds' Company Law* (4th edn). Bristol: Jordans, 2000. cxi, 753p. ISBN: 085308629X.

Davies, Paul L. *Introduction to Company Law* (Clarendon Law Series). Oxford: Oxford University Press, 2002. xxiii, 312p. ISBN: 0199249407.

De Lacey, John (ed.). *The Reform of United Kingdom Company Law*. London: Cavendish, 2002. xlvi, 503p. ISBN: 1859416934.

Dignam, Alan J. and Allen, David. *Company Law and the Human Rights Act 1998*. London: Butterworths, 2000. xlii, 360p. ISBN: 0406930309.

Dine, Janet. *Company Law* (Sweet & Maxwell's Textbook Series). London: Sweet & Maxwell, 2001. xxiii, 265p. ISBN: 0421652802.

French, Derek (ed.). *Blackstone's Statutes on Company Law*. London: Blackstone Press.

Annual.

Griffin, Stephen. *Company Law: Fundamental Principles* (3rd edn). Harlow: Longman, 2000. xli, 386p. ISBN: 0273642219.

Hannigan, Brenda M. *Annotated Guide to the Companies Act*. London: Butterworths, 2001. lxxii, 1,489p. ISBN: 0406988641.

James, Jennifer. *Company Law* (4th edn, Cavendish Publishing Questions and Answers Series). London: Cavendish, 2003. xx, 277p. ISBN: 1859417353.

Keenan, Denis. *Smith and Keenan's Company Law* (12th edn). Harlow: Longman, 2002. xxviii, 568p. ISBN: 0582473152.

Previous edition published as: *Smith and Keenan's Company Law for Students*.

Keenan, Denis. *Smith and Keenan's Company Law* (12th edn, Scottish edn). Harlow: Longman, 2002. xxviii, 603p. ISBN: 0582473160.

With Scottish supplement by Josephine R. Bisacre.

Lowry, John and Watson, Loraine. *Company Law* (Butterworths Core Text Series). London: Butterworths, 2001. xl, 469p. ISBN: 0406932433.

Mayson, Stephen, French, Derek and Ryan, Christopher. *Mayson, French and Ryan on Company Law* (19th edn). Oxford: Oxford University Press, 2002. xcii, 806p. ISBN: 0199255385.

Twentieth edition to be published (see publisher's website *http://www.oup.com*).

Morse, Geoffrey. *Partnership Law* (5th edn). London: Blackstone Press, 2001. 312p. ISBN: 1841741981.

Covers recent decisions and limited liability partnership.

Ottley, Michael. *Briefcase on Company Law* (2nd edn, Cavendish Briefcase). London: Cavendish, 2002. xxii, 157p. ISBN: 1859416993.

Pettet, B.G. *Company Law* (Longman Law Series). Harlow: Longman, 2001. 460p. ISBN: 0582077168.

Ridley, Ann. *Company Law* (Key Facts). London: Hodder & Stoughton, 2002. xii, 116p. ISBN: 0340845864.

Sealy, L.S. *Cases and Materials in Company Law* (7th edn). London: Butterworths, 2001. xxxv, 680p. ISBN: 0406929599.

Tolley's Company Law Service. London: Tolley.
Subscription with updated CD-Roms.

Walmsley, Keith (consultant ed.). *Butterworths Company Law Handbook.* London: Butterworths.
Annual.

Wareham, Robert. *Tolley's Company Law Handbook.* London: Tolley.
Annual.

Whittaker, John and Machell, John. *Limited Liability Partnerships: The New Law.* Bristol: Jordans, 2001. xli, 323p. ISBN: 0853086397.

Young, Simon. *Tolley's Limited Liability Partnerships Handbook.* London: Tolley, 2001. xix, 382p. ISBN: 0754511812.

Law reports

British Company Cases. Bicester: Croner.CCH. ISSN: 0269-0535 (BCC).
Available on *Westlaw.*

Butterworths Company Law Cases. London: Butterworths.
ISBN: 0406998582 (set) (BCLC).

Has bound volumes and loose-leaf volume.
Available on *LexisNexis Professional.*

Journals

The Company Lawyer. London: Sweet & Maxwell in association with the British Institute of Securities Laws. ISSN: 0144-1027 (Comp Law).

Available on *Westlaw.*

PLC: Practical Law for Companies Active in the UK. London: Legal and Commercial Publishing. ISSN: 0959-9940.

Websites

Companies House (http://www.companieshouse.gov.uk)

There is general information about Companies House and what it does. It is possible to search by company name.

28

Business law

New areas are the legal ramifications of e-commerce and the increasing internationalisation of business. Important recent statutes include the Competition Act 2000, the Contracts (Rights of Third Parties) Act 1999, the Financial Services and Markets Act 2000 and the Data Protection Act 1998.

Books

United Kingdom law

Abbott, Keith and Pendlebury, Norman. *Business Law* (6th edn, with amendments). London: Continuum, 2000. xv, 480p. ISBN: 0826453848.

Adams, Alix. *Law for Business Students* (2nd edn). London: Butterworths, 2000. xxii, 385p. ISBN: 0582423317.

Barrett, Brenda (ed.). *Principles of Business Law*. London: Thomson Learning, 2001. xxii, 313p. ISBN: 1861525753.

Bradgate, Robert. *Commercial Law* (3rd edn). London: Butterworths, 2000. lxi, 937p. ISBN: 0406916039.

Brown, Ian. *Commercial Law*. London: Butterworths, 2000. lxxxix, 947p. ISBN: 0406024340.

Chatterjee, Charles. *E-commerce Law for Business Managers*. Canterbury: Financial World, 2002. xxvii, 327p. ISBN: 0852975643.

Colman, Anthony D., Lyon, Victor and Hopkins, Philippa. *The Practice and Procedure of the Commercial Court* (5th edn). London: Lloyd's of London Press, 2000. xxvi, 308p. ISBN: 1859783007.

Cracknell, D.G. *Commercial Law* (3rd edn, Cracknell's Statutes). London: Old Bailey Press, 2002. xix, 604p. ISBN: 1858364728.

Previous edition by Chris Shepherd, 1998.

Craig, William J. *Taxation of E-commerce: Fiscal Regulation of the Internet* (2nd edn, Tolley's E-commerce Series). Croydon: Tolley, 2001. x, 257p. ISBN: 0754512134.

Edwards, Lilian and Waelde, Charlotte (eds). *Law and the Internet: A Framework for Electronic Commerce* (2nd edn). Oxford: Hart, 2000. xxxvii, 396p. ISBN: 1841131415.

Griffiths, Margaret and Griffiths, Ivor. *Commercial Law* (2nd edn). London: Old Bailey Press, 2001. xxxviii, 502p. ISBN: 1858363985.

Hickey, Julian J.B. et al. *E-commerce Law, Business and Tax Planning* (2nd edn). Bristol: Jordans, 2000. xxxviii, 315p. ISBN: 0853085625.

Fourth edition to be published (see publisher's website: *http://www.jordan publishing.co.uk*).

Kelly, David, Holmes, Ann and Hayward, Ruth. *Business Law* (4th edn). London: Cavendish, 2002. lxxii, 614p. ISBN: 1859417302.

Lubbock, Mark and Krosch, Louise. *A Practical Guide to E-commerce* (Legal Guidance Series). London: Stationery Office, 2000. 74p. ISBN: 0117023922.

Short guide to electronic commerce.

MacIntyre, Ewan. *Business Law.* Harlow: Longman, 2001. xli, 764p. ISBN: 0273643711.

Wide-ranging coverage of business law, including general material on the courts and legal system as well as looking at contracts, agency, torts, company law and business regulation, among others.

Marsh, S.B. and Soulsby, J. *Business Law* (8th edn). Cheltenham: Nelson Thornes, 2002. xix, 355p. ISBN: 0748766472.

Merritt, Jonathan. *Introduction to Business Law* (2nd edn). Liverpool: Academic Press, 2002. 496p. ISBN: 1903499046.

Previous edition by Arthur Lewis.

Merritt, Jonathan. *Modern Business Law: Principles and Practice.* Liverpool: Academic Press, 2002. xx, 426p. ISBN: 1903499070.

Previous edition by Arthur Lewis. Has comprehensive coverage of business law, including European, employment and e-commerce law.

Singleton, Susan. *Ecommerce: A Practical Guide to the Law.* Aldershot: Gower, 2001. xiii, 139p. ISBN: 0566082764.

Smith, Kenneth and Keenan, Denis. *Smith and Keenan's Advanced Business Law* (11th edn). Harlow: Longman, 2000. ISBN: 027364601X.

New edition to be published as *Smith and Keenan's Law for Business* (see publisher's website: *http://www.pearsoneduc.com/*).

Wegenek, Robert, O'Neill, Ged and Moore, Jonathan. *Hammond Suddards Edge: E-commerce: A Guide to the Law of Electronic Business* (3rd edn). London: Butterworths, 2002. xi, 585p. ISBN: 0406948798.

European law

Albors-Llorens, Albertina. *EC Competition Law and Policy*. Cullompton: Willan, 2002. xxvi, 164p. ISBN: 1903240743.

Bellamy, Sir Christopher and Child, Graham. *European Community Law of Competition* (5th edn). London: Sweet & Maxwell, 2001. 2v. ISBN: 0421564407.

Revised edition of *Common Market Law of Competition*. 1993.

Korah, Valentine. *Cases and Materials on EC Competition Law* (2nd edn). Oxford: Hart, 2001. xxii, 687p. ISBN: 1841133000.

Korah, Valentine. *An Introductory Guide to EC Competition Law and Practice* (7th edn). Oxford: Hart, 2000. lix, 419p. ISBN: 1841131407.

Lane, Robert. *EC Competition Law*. Harlow: Longman, 2000. xxxv, 380p. ISBN: 0582289769.

Ritter, Lennart, Braun, W. David and Rawlinson, Francis. *EC Competition Law: A Practitioner's Guide* (2nd edn, Student edn). The Hague: Kluwer Law International, 2000. xcix, 963p. ISBN: 9041113347.

Whish, Richard. *Competition Law* (4th edn). London: Butterworths, 2001. lxxix, 913p. ISBN: 0406002665.

Fifth edition to be published (see publisher's website *http://www.butterworths.co.uk*).

Law reports

The All England Law Reports. Commercial Cases. London: Butterworths. ISSN: 1470-5303.

The All England Commercial Cases consist of four loose parts a year, making up two bound volumes, covering contract, insurance, shipping and banking and other areas of commercial law.

CMLR Antitrust Reports. London: Sweet & Maxwell. ISSN: 0953-4423.

This companion series to *Common Market Law Reports* started in 1988.

E-commerce Law Reports. London: Cecile Park. ISSN: 1474-5771.

Also available as an Internet subscription.

United Kingdom Competition Law Reports. Bristol: Jordans. ISSN: 1467-7784.

Journals

Journal of Business Law. London: Sweet & Maxwell. ISSN: 0021-9460.

Available on *Westlaw*.

Online services

Corporate Law Direct

Subscription service and part of *Butterworths LexisNexis Direct Services*.

Payroll Direct

Also part of *Butterworths LexisNexis Direct Services*, this includes the law on wages and online versions of Tolley's payroll publications.

Pensions Pro

Another part of *Butterworths LexisNexis Direct Services*.

Websites

Legal Week (*http://www.legalweek.net*)

The web version of the business law journal has articles and job information. There is a free e-mail service.

The journal is on *LexisNexis*.

29

Consumer law

Major problems are car 'clocking', that is misrepresentation, and counterfeiting and trade mark infringements. European Union law is a big influence in this area with directives on marketing practices, the implementation of the Guarantees Directive marking the biggest change in consumer law for twenty years.

Books

Atiyah, P.S. *The Sale of Goods* (10th edn). Harlow: Longman, 2001. xlii, 577p. ISBN: 0582423619.

Has section on Scottish law by Hector MacQueen.

Cranston, Ross, Black, Julia and Scott, Colin. *Consumers and the Law* (Law in Context). London: Butterworths, 2000. 440p. ISBN: 0406988021.

Dobson, Paul. *Sale of Goods and Consumer Credit* (6th edn). London: Sweet & Maxwell, 2000. 512p. ISBN: 0421722304.

Includes international developments.

Guest, A.G. *Benjamin's Sale of Goods* (6th edn, The Common Law Library). London: Sweet & Maxwell, 2002. ccxxvi, 2,078p. ISBN: 0421729503.

Covers e-commerce, including the formation of electronic contracts.

Harvey, Brian W. and Parry, Deborah L. *The Law of Consumer Protection and Fair Trading* (6th edn). London: Butterworths, 2000. xxxii, 497p. ISBN: 0406930627.

Leder, M.J. and Shears, Peter. *Consumer Law* (4th edn, M&E Handbook Series). London: M. & E., 1996. xxii, 228p. ISBN: 071210870X.

Lowe, Robert and Woodruffe, Geoffrey. *Consumer Law and Practice* (5th edn). London: Sweet & Maxwell, 1999. xxxii, 447p. ISBN: 042167170X.

Sixth edition to be published (see publisher's website: *http://www.smlawpub .co.uk*).

Oughton, David and Lowry, John. *Textbook on Consumer Law*. London: Blackstone Press, 2000. 586p. ISBN: 1841740225.

Rose, Francis. *Blackstone's Statutes on Commercial and Consumer Law*. Oxford: Oxford University Press.

Aimed at undergraduates, this covers statutory instruments as well as statutes for commercial and consumer law in England and Wales. Annual.

Thomas, W.H. (ed.). *Encyclopedia of Consumer Law*. London: Sweet & Maxwell. Loose-leaf. ISBN: 0421253207.

Has consumer law legislation with annotations. Covers Office of Fair Trading circulars and European Union law.

Journals

Journal of Consumer Policy. Dordrecht: Kluwer. ISSN: 0342-5843.

Websites

Office of Fair Trading (*http://www.oft.gov.uk/default.htm*)

Has news, consumer and business information and details of market investigations.

Trading Standards (*http://www.tradingstandards.net*)

Has consumer protection advice and trading standards information, as well as the annotated versions of legislation in this area. Includes contact details for relevant organisations.

30

Banking and financial services

The Financial Services and Markets Act 2000 overhauled the regulatory system for banking, financial services and insurance. The Financial Services Authority was set up as the main regulator, with a statutory Financial Ombudsman Service to settle financial disputes and a Financial Compensation Scheme to unify arrangements for compensation.

Other new developments affecting banking and financial services law include the European Central Bank and e-money. Banking and financial services also face worries over money laundering and terrorist financing.

Books

United Kingdom law

Abrams, Charles. *A Short Guide to the Financial Services and Markets Act 2000*. Bicester: CCH.New Law, 2000. 57p. ISBN: 0863255604.

Ashurst, Morris, Crisp (firm). *The Financial Services and Markets Act: A Practical Legal Guide*. London: Sweet & Maxwell, 2001. xliii, 425p. ISBN: 0421679905.

Blair, Michael et al. *Blackstone's Guide to the Financial Services and Markets Act 2000*. London: Blackstone Press, 2001. 583p. ISBN: 1841741167.

Looks at the new regulatory system, which affects banking, insurance and other investment services. There is background information on the Act and coverage of the subordinate legislation.

Butterworths Financial Regulation Service. London: Butterworths. Loose-leaf. ISBN: 0406931402.

Cranston, Ross. *Principles of Banking Law* (2nd edn). Oxford: Oxford University Press, 2002. xliii, 470p. ISBN: 0199253315.

Includes developments under the Financial Services and Markets Act 2002. Covers international and cross-border banking.

Ellinger, E.P., Lomnicka, Eva Z. and Hooley, Richard. *Modern Banking Law* (3rd edn). Oxford: Oxford University Press, 2002. 839p. ISBN: 0199248311.

Looks at the law relating to a wide spectrum of banking organisations. Examines different types of loan and credit agreements, syndicated lending and recovery of mistaken payments.

Ferran, Eilas and Goodhart, Charles A.E. (eds). *Regulating Financial Services and Markets in the Twenty First Century*. Oxford: Hart, 2001. 345p. ISBN: 1841132799.

Grier, Nicholas. *Banking Law in Scotland* (Greens Practice Library). Edinburgh: W. Green, 2001. xxxiii, 284p. ISBN: 0414013093.

Hapgood, Mark (ed.). *Paget's Law of Banking* (12th edn). London: Butterworths, 2002. cxvi, 830p. ISBN: 0406913439.

The first new edition since 1996 covers 200 new cases, the effects of the Civil Procedure Rules and the Financial Services and Markets Act 2000, the 2001 banking code and the 2002 business banking code.

Haynes, Andrew (ed.). *Butterworths Financial Services Law Guide*. London: Butterworths, 2002. xxvi, 463p. ISBN: 0406939136.

King, Richard. *Gutteridge and Megrah's Law of Bankers' Commercial Credits* (8th edn). London: Europa, 2001. 423p. ISBN: 185743112X.

Lomnicka, Eva Z. and Powell, John L. *Encyclopedia of Financial Services Law*. London: Sweet & Maxwell. Loose-leaf. ISBN: 0421368802.

McMeel, Gerard and Virgo, John. *Financial Advice and Financial Products: Law and Liability.* Oxford: Oxford University Press, 2001. lxvi, 925p. ISBN: 0198268238.

Looks at the liability of financial advisors in the light of the Financial Services and Markets Act 2000 and the Equitable Life case.

Norton, Joseph J. and Walker, George A. *Banks, Fraud and Crime* (2nd edn). London: LLP, 2000. xxxii, 465p. ISBN: 1859785506.

Perry, James (ed.). *The Financial Services and Markets Act: A Practical Legal Guide.* London: Sweet & Maxwell, 2001. xliii, 425p. ISBN: 0421679905.

Roberts, Graham. *Law Relating to Financial Services* (4th edn). Canterbury: Financial World, 2001. xxii, 418p. ISBN: 0852976186.

Rutledge, G. Philip and Haines, Jason D. *Electronic Markets* (Butterworths Compliance Series). London: Butterworths, 2001. xiii, 397p. ISBN: 0406937508.

The legal aspects of electronic financial services.

Sabalot, Deborah (consultant ed.). *Butterworths Financial Services Law Handbook* (4th edn). London: Butterworths, 2002. xiii, 1,585p. ISBN: 0406931402.

Sabalot, Deborah and Whittaker, Andrew. *A Guide to the Financial Services and Markets Act 2000.* London: Butterworths, 2002. 400p. ISBN: 0406931410.

Savla, Sandeep. *Money Laundering and Financial Intermediaries* (Studies in Comparative Corporate and Financial Law, Vol. 8). The Hague and London: Kluwer Law International, 2001. xviii, 233p. ISBN: 9041197958.

Wadsley, Joan and Penn, Graham. *The Law Relating to Domestic Banking* (2nd edn, Banking Law, Vol. 1). London: Sweet & Maxwell, 2000. lxxi, 797p. ISBN: 0421413808.

Previous edition was by Graham Penn, A.M. Shea and A. Arora. 1987.

European law

Usher, J.A. *The Law of Money and Financial Services in the EC* (2nd edn). Oxford: Oxford University Press, 2000. xliv, 255p. ISBN: 0198298773.

Law reports

Lloyd's Law Reports: Banking. London: LLP. ISSN: 1461-8532.

Continues *Banking Law Reports.*

Journals

Banking Law Update. London: Butterworths.

Butterworths Journal of International Banking and Financial Law. London: Butterworths. ISSN: 0269-2694.

Journal of International Banking Law. Oxford: ESC. ISSN: 0267-937X.

Online services

Banking Law Direct

Part of *Butterworths LexisNexis Direct Services.*

Financial Regulations Direct

Also part of *Butterworths LexisNexis Direct Services.*

Websites

Financial Ombudsman Service (*http://www.financial-ombudsman.org.uk*)

The site for the free independent service for resolving disputes with financial services firms, including insurance disputes. Has details about the service, including frequently asked questions, latest news and details of how to make a complaint.

Financial Services Authority (*http://www.fsa.gov.uk*)

Includes the online version of the *FSA Handbook of Rules and Guidance.*

Financial Services Compensation Scheme (FCSC) (*http://www.fscs.org.uk/*)

The site for the scheme paid for by the financial services industry which pays compensation to customers when the authorised firm cannot, usually because it is bankrupt. The site has information on claiming, as well as annual reports and press releases.

Global Banking Law Database (*http://www.gbld.org/index.aspx*)

Run by the World Bank and International Monetary Fund, this site has links to these organisations and to sites by jurisdiction. It might be a useful resource, but it is disappointing because of the lack of sites listed under United Kingdom.

31

Insurance law

Insurance law was affected by the overhaul of financial services under the Financial Services and Markets Act 2000. The Law Commission is currently looking at the reform of insurance contracts.

Books

Barlow, Lyde & Gilbert (firm). *Tolley's Insurance Handbook* (2nd edn). London: Tolley, 2000. 365p. ISBN: 0754507440.

Birds, John and Hird, Norma J. *Birds' Modern Insurance Law* (5th edn). London: Sweet & Maxwell, 2001. xlii, 413p. ISBN: 0421716703.

Brown, Michael (ed.). *Butterworths Insurance Law Handbook* (7th edn). London: Butterworths, 2002. xvi, 2,408p. ISBN: 0406945772.

Clarke, Malcolm A. *The Law of Insurance Contracts* (4th edn). London: LLP, 2002. cl, 1,091p. ISBN: 1843111705.

McGee, Andrew. *The Modern Law of Insurance*. London: Butterworths, 2001. liv, 765p. ISBN: 0406903859.

Merkin, Robert. *Colinvaux and Merkin's Insurance Contract Law* (new edn). London: Sweet & Maxwell. Loose-leaf. ISBN: 0421791500.

Surridge, Robert J. et al. *Houseman and Davies: Law of Life Assurance* (12th edn). London: Butterworths, 2001. xli, 658p. ISBN: 0406935890.

32

European law

European law is important in its own right and for its influence on British law. New legislation is often enacted to implement European Union directives.

Books

Annull, Anthony et al. *Wyatt and Dashwood's European Union Law* (4th edn). London: Sweet & Maxwell, 2000. cxxvii, 817p. ISBN: 0421680407.

Birtwistle, Tim. *Principles of European Law.* Bromborough: Liverpool Academic Press, 2002. vii, 179p. ISBN: 1903499038.

Coles, Joanne. *Law of the European Union: Textbook* (3rd edn). London: Old Bailey Press, 2001. xxix, 262p. ISBN: 1858364124.

Craig, Paul and De Burca, Grianne. *EU Law: Text, Cases and Materials.* Oxford: Oxford University Press, 2002. cxiv, 1,241p. ISBN: 0199249431.

Covers institutional and substantive European Union law, split equally between text and cases. Includes recent legislation, with a particular focus on the Treaty of Nice.

Cuthbert, Mike. *European Union Law* (5th edn, Cavendish Q and A Series). London: Cavendish Press, 2003. 340p. ISBN: 1859417337.

Encyclopedia of European Community Law (European Legislation Series). London: Sweet & Maxwell. Loose-leaf. ISBN: 0421207604.

Includes significant European legislation, consolidated with annotations; across the range of topics, including intellectual property, employment and competition law.

European Union Law Library. London: Sweet & Maxwell. Loose-leaf. ISBN: 0421753005.

Covers the whole range of European Union law, with concise commentary and case annotation. Also available on CD-Rom and there are choices of subscriptions.

Foster, Nigel G. (ed.). *Blackstone's EC Legislation.* Oxford: Oxford University Press.

Includes secondary as well as primary legislation. Annual.

Hunnings, Neville, Beaumont, Paul and Muir, Gordon. *Encyclopedia of European Union Law* (European Legislation Series). London: Sweet & Maxwell. Loose-leaf. ISBN: 0421534400.

Has European Union constitutional texts, including the original treaties, European association agreements and other materials. Also includes the rules of procedure of the courts and political institutions of the Union.

Lasok, K.P.E. and Lasok, D. *Law and Institutions of the European Union* (7th edn). London: Butterworths, 2001. cxxxvii, 874p. ISBN: 0406901864.

McCormick, John. *Understanding the European Union: A Concise Introduction* (2nd edn, The European Union Series). Basingstoke: Palgrave, 2002. xvi, 237p. ISBN: 033394867X.

Medhurst, David. *A Brief and Practical Guide to EU Law* (3rd edn). Oxford: Blackwell Science, 2000. 221p. ISBN: 0632051841.

Monar, Joerg and Wessels, Wolfgang. *The European Union after the Treaty of Amsterdam.* London: Continuum, 2001. 338p. ISBN: 0826447694.

Nicoll, William and Salmon, Trevor C. *Understanding the European Union.* Harlow: Longman, 2001. xxi, 572p. ISBN: 0130208388.

Paterson, Janet B. *EC Law* (Law Basics: Student Study Guides). Edinburgh: W. Green, 2002. 101p. ISBN: 0414014030.

Peterson, John and Shackleton, Michael (eds). *The Institutions of the European Union* (The New European Union Series). Oxford: Oxford University Press, 2002. xxiii, 402p. ISBN: 0198700520.

Shaw, Josephine. *Law of the European Union* (3rd edn, Palgrave Law Masters). Basingstoke: Macmillan Palgrave, 2000. lxii, 591p. ISBN: 0333924916.

Steiner, Josephine and Woods, Lorna. *Textbook on EC Law* (7th edn). London: Blackstone Press, 2000. lxxxvi, 586p. ISBN: 1841740233.

Covers the institutions and the law-making process. Also covers changes to remedies and rights to free movement.

Vincenzi, Christopher and Fairhurst, John. *Law of the European Community* (3rd edn, The Foundation Studies in Law Series). Harlow: Longman, 2002. lxxx, 496p. ISBN: 0582438136.

Weatherill, Stephen. *Cases and Materials on EC Law* (5th edn). London: Blackstone Press, 2000. lxiv, 763p. ISBN: 1841740128.

Has a range of material relating to the development of the Community and its policies, as well as important legislation and major judgments from the Court of Justice since the 1960s.

Wyatt, Derrick (ed.). *Rudden and Wyatt's EU Treaties and Legislation* (8th edn). Oxford: Oxford University Press, 2002. xxiv, 408p. ISBN: 0199249369.

Law reports

The All England Law Reports. European Cases. London: Butterworths. ISSN: 1464-5599.

The All England European Cases have decisions of the Court of Justice and the Court of First Instance in cases from European Union jurisdictions. There are ten issues a year making one volume.

Common Market Law Reports. London: Sweet & Maxwell. ISSN: 0588-7445 (CMLR).

Very comprehensive series started in 1962. A companion series is *CMLR Antitrust Reports* (see p. 185).
Available on *The Justis Databases* and *Westlaw*.

European Court Reports. Luxembourg: Office for Official Publications of the European Communities. ISSN: 1022-842X (ECR).

These are the *Reports of Cases Before the Court of Justice and the Court of First Instance.* The cases are in different volumes according to the courts.

Legislation

Official Journal of the European Communities. Luxembourg: Office for Official Publications of the European Communities (OJ Eur Comm).

Published in two main series, Legislation (L), which has adopted legislation and will be the one most wanted, and Information and Notices (C for Communications), which has a wide-range of material including draft directives and regulations, opinions, including those of the Commission, and announcements of various kinds.
L and C series are on *Eurolaw* (see p. 206), *Westlaw* (1990 onwards) and *LexisNexis Professional* (1998 onwards). The *Official Journal* is also available on CD-Rom.

Finding tools

Butterworths EC Case Citator and Service. London: Butterworths.

This was issued twice a year with a fortnightly case listing service until it ceased publication in 2002. By looking up a case by name or number, e.g. C-298/89, you are directed to the *Common Market Law Reports* or *European Court Reports*.

European Current Law: Monthly Digest. London: Sweet & Maxwell.
ISSN: 0964-0037.

European law equivalent to *Current Law Monthly Digest* providing a method
of tracking down recent cases.

European Current Law Year Book. London: Sweet & Maxwell.

Both this and the *Monthly Digest* are split into the following four sections:
Focus, with articles covering legal developments, sections on the European
Union and national jurisdictions arranged by subject headings, and finally a
reference section, including a glossary of courts and abbreviations. Included are
tables of treaties, cases reported and legislation digested. Details of legislation
recently passed, press releases issued by the European Commission and national
laws implementing European Union obligations are given. There are cumulative
tables of directives and regulations, by subject and in numerical order, supported
by indexes. Look in the subject index and you are led to an abstract. Check for
any new developments in *European Current Law: Monthly Digest.*

*Halsbury's Statutory Instruments. EC Legislation Implementator: The Guide
to the Implementation of Community Directives.* London: Butterworths.

A very useful new annual guide, with lists of the directives implemented in the
United Kingdom and their corresponding statutory instruments. There is also a
chronological table.

Finding European Union law

The electronic sources, such as *Eurolaw*, are a very powerful way of
finding European law, being right up-to-date and full-text (see p. 206). The
Eur-Lex website is also very useful (see p. 207). As an alternative, many
treaties can be found as an appendix to textbooks or in loose-leaf volumes,
such as the *Encyclopedia of European Union Law, Rudden and Wyatt's
EU Treaties and Legislation and Blackstone's EC Legislation. Halsbury's
Laws* (see p. 43) has references to relevant European Union law.

As with British law, there is a right way of citing cases and legislation and understanding the forms of citation helps with searching for material. There is an official number for decisions or opinions and directives and regulations.

A typical example of a Court of Justice case cited in the *European Court Reports* is C-186/2001, *Dory, Alexander* v. *Germany* [2001] ECR I-7823. The citation begins with the official document number and this starts with a letter for the type of action such as C for decisions of the Court of Justice. The alternatives are T, decisions of the Court of First Instance, and P for appeals from the Court of First Instance to the Court of Justice. Next is the case number, being two numbers separated by a slash, the second one being the year in which the action was started. The names of the parties are followed by the year of the *European Court Reports* in brackets, the volume number in Roman numerals and the page number of the report. Roman numeral I means cases before the Court of Justice and II cases before the Court of First Instance.

In respect of legislation, there is a difference in citation between regulations and directives.

Regulations have two numbers separated by a slash, the first being the consecutive number of the instrument and the second the year in which it was adopted. For example, the citation for a Council regulation on import values for certain fruit and vegetables is 75/2002.

Directives also have two numbers but the first is the year of adoption and the second is the consecutive number. So the citation for a Council directive on reduced rates of VAT is 2002/92.

A good means of searching for documents is to use the *Official Journal* number. Citations from the journal start with the abbreviation OJ, the year, the first letter of the series and the number in that series. An example is the Council regulation on deep-sea fishing, which is OJ 2002 L/356/1.

Details of national law implementing European law can be found in the *European Current Law Year Book* and *Monthly Digest*.

Journals

Bulletin of the European Union. Brussels: Commission of the European Communities. ISSN: 1025-4005.

Common Market Law Review. The Hague: Kluwer Law International in cooperation with the British Institute of International and Comparative Law and the Europa Instituut of the University of Leyden. ISSN: 0165-0750 (CMLR).

Available on *Kluwer Online.*

European Law Review. London: Sweet & Maxwell. ISSN: 0307-5400 (ELR).

Covers the Council of Europe and legal aspects of European integration.
Available on *Westlaw.*

Yearbook of European Law. Oxford: Clarendon Press (YBEL).

Online services

Celex (The Justis Databases)

The official full-text legal database of the European Union.

ECJ Proceedings (The Justis Databases)

Information on the judicial proceedings of the Court of Justice and the Court of First Instance, including short summaries of judgments and brief notes on opinions delivered by the Advocates-General.

EU Direct

Part of *Butterworths LexisNexis Direct Services*, this includes the full text of legislation and cases.

Eurolaw

Comprises the full-text legal database *Celex*, with additions by ILI. It has impressive coverage, with full text of the treaties setting up the Union, cases, preparatory documents, national provisions implementing European Union legislation and Parliamentary questions. Search options include legislation number, title, text, document type and OJ reference. Also included is the very useful *Spearhead Database* from the Department of Trade and Industry, with official briefings from the British government. Available through the Internet or by monthly or quarterly CD-Rom.

For more information see: *http://www.ili.co.uk/en/eurolaw.html*.

European Legal Journals Index

Available on *Current Legal Information*, this includes more than eighty English language sources for European Union law and individual European countries. The index supplies references and abstracts.

Lawtel EU

A section of *Lawtel*, this includes cases, legislation and commission reports.

LexisNexis Professional (see p. 34).

Has a European database, including the *Official Journal*.

OJ Daily (The Justis Databases)

Daily update service with table of contents of the *Official Journal* C and L series with links to the full text.

RAPID Database (The Justis Databases)

Official European press releases.

Westlaw UK (see p. 35)

Has European law, including treaties, *Official Journal* C series, Parliamentary questions and case reports.

Websites

Council of Europe Site on Treaties (*http://conventions.coe.int*)

The Treaty Office site has full texts of the treaties.

Court of Justice of the European Communities (*http://www.europa.eu.int/cj/en/index.htm*)

Has texts of the judgments, opinions and orders of the Court of First Instance since June 1997 as read out in court. In addition, the site has news, a diary, research tools, including a digest of Community case law, alphabetical and subject indexes, annotations of the judgments and relevant links.

ELSA Law Web (*http://www.elsa.org/research/lawweb.asp*)

Part of the site run by the European Law Students' Association, *ELSA Law Web* is a searchable collection of links to European Union institutions and to the law and legal systems of mainly European countries.

Eur-Lex: The Portal to European Union Law (*http://europa.eu.int/eur-lex*)

Part of the *Europa* site, this is an attempt to publish the whole body of European Union law. It has links to the *Official Journal*, treaties, legislation, legislation in preparation, case law, Parliamentary questions, documents of public interest and *Celex*.

Europa: The European Union On-line (*http://www.europa.eu.int*)

Packed with information about the institutions of the European Union, this site has news, a section called *EU at a Glance*, information sources and links to the sites of the individual institutions. There are also links to official publications, including treaties, the European Parliament, the *Bulletin of the European Union* and the *Official Journal Online*.

International law

Books

Brownlie, Ian (ed.). *Basic Documents in International Law.* Oxford: Oxford University Press, 2002. xi, 341p. ISBN: 0199249423.

Source of important documents across the different elements of international law.

Brownlie, Ian. *Principles of Public International Law* (5th edn). Oxford: Oxford University Press, 1998. 743p. ISBN: 0198762984.

Cassese, Antonio. *International Criminal Law.* Oxford: Oxford University Press, 2003. lvi, 472p. ISBN: 0199259119.

The former President of the International Criminal Tribunal for the Former Yugoslavia looks at the principles governing international crimes and international court trials. Includes relevant English cases, with translations of Dutch, French, German, Israeli, Italian and Spanish cases. There is a companion website.

Cassese, Antonio. *International Law.* Oxford: Oxford University Press, 2001. xvii, 469p. ISBN: 0198299982.

The history and latest developments of international law and its dynamics. A companion website acts as an online casebook, having documents relating to the text, as well as links to relevant websites.

Dixon, Martin. *Textbook on International Law* (4th edn). London: Blackstone Press, 2000. xxx, 356p. ISBN: 1854318942.

Looks at the current position, the decisions of international courts and tribunals and proposals for reform. Supported by the casebook, McCorquodale, Robert and Dixon, Martin, *Cases and Materials on International Law*.

Evans, Malcolm D. *Blackstone's International Law Documents* (5th edn, Blackstone's Statute Books). London: Blackstone Press, 2001. vi, 558p. ISBN: 1841742678.

Sixth edition to be published (see publisher's website *http://www.oup.com*).

Klabbers, Ian. *An Introduction to International Institutional Law*. Cambridge: Cambridge University Press, 2002. xxxviii, 399p. ISBN: 0521520932.

An analysis of international institutional law, including the law relating to finance, treaty-making and dispute settlement.

McCorquodale, Robert and Dixon, Martin. *Cases and Materials on International Law* (4th edn). Oxford: Oxford University Press, 2003. xxviii, 628p. ISBN: 0199259992.

A collection for students of important documents and a companion to Martin Dixon's *Textbook on International Law*.

Malanczuk, Peter. *Akehurst's Modern Introduction to International Law* (8th edn). London: Routledge, 2001. 504p. ISBN: 0415243556.

Previously published as: *A Modern Introduction to International Law*.

Simpson, Gerry (ed.). *The Nature of International Law* (The Library of Essays in International Law). Aldershot: Ashgate, 2001. xxxvii, 640p. ISBN: 0754620654.

Law reports

International Law Reports. Cambridge: Cambridge University Press/Grotius (ILR).

Continues: *Annual Digest and Reports of Public International Law Cases*. Has consolidated tables of cases.

Journals

American Journal of International Law. Washington, DC: American Society of International Law. ISSN: 0002-9300 (AJIL).

British Yearbook of International Law. London: Oxford University Press for Royal Institute of International Affairs. ISSN: 0068-2691 (BYBIL).
A mixture of articles and in-depth surveys on international law.

Canadian Yearbook of International Law. Vancouver: University of British Columbia Press. ISSN: 0069-0058 (Can YBIL).

European Journal of International Law. Oxford: Oxford University Press. ISSN: 0938-5428 (EJIL).

Has articles, including occasional symposia, a current developments section and book reviews. The journal is supported by a website (*http://www.ejil.org*), which has material complementing the printed work.

International and Comparative Law Quarterly. Oxford: Oxford University Press [for] the British Institute of International and Comparative Law. ISSN: 0020-5893 (ICLQ).

Covers comparative, public and private international law. Has articles on European law and on human rights.
Available on *LexisNexis Professional.*

International Legal Materials. Washington, DC: American Society of International Law. ISSN: 0020-7829 (ILM).

Reproduces texts of documents, chosen for present and future legal significance, covering the broad scope of international law. Includes treaties, cases and reports from the UN and other bodies. Covers international organisations, jurisdiction, maritime law and trade, e-commerce, environmental law, human rights and war crimes jurisprudence. Current and recent contents are available on the Society's website: *http://www.asil.org/ilmtoc.pdf.*

The materials are now also available as *ILM on CD-Rom*, as well as being on *LexisNexis Professional*.

Finding tools

General Index to Treaty Series: 1907–1911. London: HMSO, 1912.

Websites

Foreign and Commonwealth Office Documents Database (Treaties Section)
(*http://www.fco.gov.uk/servlet/Front?pagename=OpenMarket/Xcelerate/
ShowPage&c=Page&cid=1007029396014*)

Has pdf files of records of all bilateral and multilateral treaties involving the United Kingdom. Includes notes on status.

International Court of Justice (*http://www.icj-cij.org*)

Includes news, basic documents relating to the court, lists of cases being heard, the full text of cases from 1996 and summaries of earlier cases.

United Nations (*http://www.un.org*)

Has news and information about the UN, its structure, main bodies and member states.

World Law (International Section)
(*http://www.worldlii.org/hosted_databases.html#int*)

Easy way to search for links to international organisations.

Appendix

Legal publishers and Internet bookshops

Legal publishers

Two American-run websites supply a list of law publishers with links to their sites:

AcqWeb (*http://www.library.vanderbilt.edu/law/acqs/pubr/law.html*)

Findlaw (*http://www.findlaw.com/04publications/index.htm*)

List of major legal publishers

Blackstone Press – *see Oxford University Press*

Butterworths – *see LexisNexis Butterworths Tolley*

Cavendish (*http://www.cavendishpublishing.com*)
The Glass House
Wharton Street
London
WC1X 9PX
Tel: 020 7278 8000
      020 7278 8080
E-mail: *info@cavendishpublishing.com*

Independent law publisher has online catalogue, browsable by topic as well as searchable for a known title. It now offers all its law books as e-books in its 'elibrary'. Cavendish is advanced in supporting many of its textbooks with companion sites, particularly for contract, business and constitutional and administrative law. It is possible to send authors questions. Students may also find the revision tips and self-assessment questions useful.

Chambers and Partners Publishing
Saville House
23 Long Lane
London
EC1A 9HL
Tel: 020 7606 1300

Context (*http://www.context.co.uk*)
Grand Union House
20 Kentish Town Road
London
NW1 9NR
Tel: 020 7267 8989
E-mail: *webmaster@context.co.uk*

Publishes legal, business and official information.

Croner CCH Group (*http://www.croner.cch.co.uk*)
Croner House
145 London Road
Kingston upon Thames
Surrey
KT2 6SR
Tel: 020 8547 3333
E-mail: *info@croner.cch.co.uk*

Ellis Publications (*http://www.ellispub.com*)
PO Box 1059
6201 BB Maastrict
NL
Tel: +31 (0)43 321 5313

European Union law publisher.

EMIS Professional Publishing Limited (*http://www.emispp.com*)
31–33 Stonehills House
Howards Gate
Welwyn Garden City
Hertfordshire
AL8 6PU
Tel: 01707 334823
E-mail: *sales@emispp.com*

Europa Law Publishing (*http://www.europalawpublishing.com*)
PO Box 6047
9702 HA Groningen
The Netherlands
Tel: 3150 526 3844
E-mail: *info@europalawpublishing.com*

Family Law – see *Jordan Publishing* for contact details (*http://www.familylaw
.co.uk/flhome.nsfl*)

Hart Publishing (*http://www.hartpub.co.uk*)
Salter's Boatyard
Folly Bridge
Abingdon Road
Oxford
OX1 4LB
Tel: 01865 245533
E-mail: *mail@hartpub.co.uk*

Incorporated Council of Law Reporting for England and Wales (ICLR)
(*http://www.lawreports.co.uk*)
Megarry House
119 Chancery Lane
London
WC2A 1PP
Tel: 020 7242 6471
E-mail: *postmaster@iclr.co.uk*

Informa Professional Publishing (*http://www.informa.com*)
Customer Services
Sheepen Place
Colchester
Essex
CO3 3LP
Tel: 01206 772 223
E-mail: *Professional.enquiries@informa.com*

John Murray (*http://62.173.95.217/jmurray/home.asp*)
50 Albemarle Street
London
W15 4BD
Tel: 020 7493 4361
E-mail: *enquiries@johnmurrays.co.uk*

Jordan Publishing Limited (*http://www.jordanpublishing.co.uk*)
21 St Thomas Street
Bristol
BS1 6JS
Tel: 0117 923 0600
E-mail: *customerservice@jordanpublishing.co.uk*

Includes Family Law imprint.

Kluwer Law International (*http://www.kluwerlaw.com*)
Sterling House
66 Wilton Road
London
SW1V 1DE
Tel: 020 7233 5729
E-mail: *enquiries@kluwerlaw.co.uk*

Law Pack Publishing (*http://www.lawpack.co.uk*)
77–89 Alscot Road
London
SE1 3AW
Tel: 020 7394 4040
E-mail: *mailbox@lawpack.co.uk*

Specialist in self-help legal books.

Law Society Publishing (*http://www.publishing.lawsociety.org.uk*)
113 Chancery Lane
London
WC2A 1PI
Tel: 020 7316 5599
E-mail: *publishing@lawsociety.org.uk*

Legal Action Group (*http://www.lag.org.uk*)
242 Pentonville Road
London
N1 9UN
Tel: 020 7837 6094
E-mail: *lag@lag.org.uk*

LexisNexis Butterworths Tolley (*http://www.butterworths.co.uk*)
Halsbury House
35 Chancery Lane
London
WC2A 1EL
Tel: 020 7400 2500

The site has an online catalogue and bookshop.

The publisher is redesigning its website to be more in line with *http://www .lexisnexis.co.uk*. The latter has the useful zone called *Law Campus* with a choice of student, lecturer, librarian and bookseller focus. There are regular updates on popular books and new legislation and case law arranged by subject area.

Old Bailey Press (*http://www.holborncollege.ac.uk/OldBaileyPress.cfm*)
Woolwich Road
Charlton
London
SE7 8LN
Tel: 020 8317 6039
E-mail: *obp@hltpublications.co.uk*

The publication division of Holborn College.

Oxford University Press (*http://www.oup.com*)
Great Clarendon Street
Oxford
OX2 6DP
Tel: 01865 556767
Email: *law@oup.co.uk*

Owns Blackstone Press.

Palladian Law Publishing (*http://www.palladianlaw.com*)
Beach Road
Bembridge
Isle of Wight
PO35 5NQ
Tel: 01983 872574
E-mail: *palladian@compuserve.com*

Sweet & Maxwell (*http://www.smlawpub.co.uk*)
100 Avenue Road
London
NW3 3PF
Tel: 020 7393 7000
E-mail: *customer.services@sweetandmaxwell.co.uk*

Tolleys – see *LexisNexis Butterworths Tolley*

TSO (The Stationery Office) (*http://www.tso.co.uk*)

The website has links to the Stationery Office bookshop where you can order any British book in print. There is a search facility and lists of official publications (not that comprehensive), the Daily List and lists by subject area.

W. Green (*http://www.wgreen.co.uk*)
21 Alva Street
Edinburgh
EH2 4PS
Tel: 0131 225 4879
E-mail: *enquiries@wgreen.co.uk*

Scottish law publisher, part of Sweet & Maxwell.

W.S. Hein & Co. Inc. (*http://www.wshein.com*)
1285 Main Street
Buffalo
NY
14209-1987
USA
Tel: (+1-716) 882-2600
E-mail: *mail@wshein.com*

Source for the first 99 volumes of the publications of the Selden Society.

Waterlow Professional Publishing (*http://www.waterlow.com*)
Paulton House
8 Shepherdess Walk
London
N1 7LB
Tel: 020 7490 0049

Publisher of directories and of the *ConnectingLegal* website.

Internet bookshops

Amazon (*http://www.amazon.co.uk*)

Has books on law, business and finance. Includes new and future publications, and second-hand law books are available from Amazon Marketplace, although only consider buying the latest editions.

Hammicks Legal Bookshops Online (*http://www.hammickslegal.com*)

This is the website of the specialist legal bookseller, with news and updates on legal publishing as well as listings of available stock. There is also an occasional newsletter by e-mail which has details of latest publications.

Internet Bookshop (*http://www.internetbookshop.co.uk*)

Part of W.H. Smith, the Internet Bookshop is popular with librarians and law has its own section.

Lawyer's Professional Book Services (*http://www.lawbooks.freeserve.co.uk*)

Run by Berridge Law, this site highlights new titles by subject and has new book previews.

Wildy (*http://www.wildy.com*)

This is *Webs Web*, the independent electronic bookshop for law run by Wildy. As well as covering backruns and out-of-print books, it also includes new books and you can subscribe to Wildy's book news, sent by post or e-mail.

Indexes

Index of online services

Index of websites

Acas
  (*http://www.acas.org.uk*), 105
Access to Justice Final Report
  (*http://www.law.warwick.ac.uk/woolf/report/*), 132
AcqWeb
  (*http://www.library.vanderbilt.edu/law/acqs/pubr/law.html*), 213
Acts of the UK Parliament
  (*http://www.hmso.gov.uk/acts.htm*), 20
AHRB Research Centre for Studies in Intellectual Property and Technology Law
  (*http://www.law.ed.ac.uk/ahrb/*), 171
Amazon
  (*http://www.amazon.co.uk*), 220
Association of Law Teachers (ALT)
  (*http://www.lawteacher.ac.uk*), 50
Association of Personal Injury Lawyers
  (*http://www.apil.com*), 151
Asylum Support Information: Your Resource for Asylum Support Information
  (*http://www.asylumsupport.info/*), 93
BAILII (British and Irish Legal Information Institute)
  (*http://www.bailii.org*), 38
Bar Council
  (*http://www.barcouncil.org.uk*), 57
Bar Directory
  (*http://www.smlawpub.co.uk/online/bardirectory/login/login.cfm*), 57
BIALL (British and Irish Association of Law Librarians)
  (*www.biall.org.uk*), 50

Index of authors, editors and contributors

Index of titles

Alphabetical list of the law reports, journals and books by title.

Printed in the United Kingdom
by Lightning Source UK Ltd.
113740UKS00001B/4-21